Spirit of the Mind

**"And be renewed
in the spirit of your mind"
Ephesians 4:23**

Spirit of the Mind

**"And be renewed
in the spirit of your mind"
Ephesians 4:23**

by
Casey Treat

Harrison House
Tulsa, Oklahoma

Unless otherwise indicated, all Scripture quotations are taken from the *King James Version* of the Bible.

2nd Printing
Over 15,000 in Print

Spirit of the Mind —
Unlocking the Mysteries of the Subconscious
ISBN 0-89274-561-4
Copyright © 1989 by Casey Treat Ministries
P. O. Box 98800
Seattle, Washington 98198

Published by Harrison House, Inc.
P. O. Box 35035
Tulsa, Oklahoma 74153

Contents

Introduction

Have you ever wondered why many "good" Christians sin? why "good" Christians backslide? why "good" Christian marriages fail?

In my book, *Renewing the Mind: The Arena for Success*, I go into much detail about the process of renewing the mind. There is yet another step we must take if we are to continue in our growth with the Lord. Paul said in Ephesians 4:24, **Be renewed in the spirit of your mind.** The Bible teaches that the spirit of your mind can drag you back to the behavior of the "old man." That old lifestyle can take over again unless you have renewed the spirit of your mind.

As you read through these chapters of *Spirit of the Mind*, do not just read looking for interesting information. Examine those areas of your life that have been difficult, limiting or negative, and see how you can begin to change the spirit of your mind in those areas. I pray you will go through this process with me so you can have God's best in every area of your life. Do not be like I used to be, and like so many Christians are today — stuck in the mud, spinning their wheels and going nowhere.

* * *

I remember thinking, "Be cool, drive carefully, and don't attract any attention to yourself" as I drove south on Interstate 5 on my way home to Tacoma. I had smoked a few joints and taken some other drugs, but

I knew what was going on. I also knew if I could just stay awake, I would be home in a few minutes.

Little did I realize that even while those thoughts were going through my mind, I had gone unconscious and driven the car into the median dividing the north and south lanes. My car sat stuck deep in the mud, wheels turning at 55 miles per hour, going nowhere. God only knows how long I sat there flinging mud into the air, all the while thinking I was being careful not to attract any attention to myself. The next thing I remember was the flashing of lights and a man's voice yelling at me to turn the car off. At first I wondered why he was so upset. Then I realized, "Oh, no, not again! I have blown it one more time." I knew what the results would be.

It did not take the officer long to conclude that I was loaded, and we headed for the Pierce County Jail. I had been through the routine four or five times before: pictures, prints, strip search — then into the tank. The feelings were always the same — emptiness, hurt, fear, anger, and every other negative emotion imaginable. I spent that night in jail and started the process of trying to get out the next day.

Why would a nineteen-year-old kid put himself through this time and time again?

Why did I want to stay loaded twenty-four hours a day?

Why, when my life was not *that* bad, was I so willing to throw everything away?

Since I had been in jail several times already, I was given a choice this time to either go to a state penitentiary for a maximum of one year, or go to the Washington Drug Rehabilitation Center. I knew I did not want prison, so I chose the drug rehabilitation center. I hid as many drugs as I could into the lining of my clothes before I left. I was nineteen years old, depressed, scared and all alone. I felt like I was old enough to die, and I was afraid that if I did die, eternity might be worse.

Not long after I entered the center, I realized the people there were different. They had a spirit, a joy, and a freedom I had not seen in any "square" person before. I wanted it — I had been looking for that freedom for years. I turned in my drugs and began to learn a new lifestyle.

I soon discovered that these people were all born again and baptized with the Holy Spirit. I did not know what that meant, but if that was what made them so happy, I wanted it. In November of 1974 I, too, was born again. Jesus became the Lord of my life. I was also filled with His Spirit and began to pray in other tongues. A tremendous peace, joy and liberty came into my life. I had become a Christian.

At first I thought all Christians had it "all together," never had a problem, and lived "happily ever after." It did not take long to realize this was not the case. Many of the drug rehabilitation residents, who had been saved and filled with the spirit, ended up back on the streets in worse condition than before. I saw church members still bound in fear, bitterness, depression and other problems.

After twenty-one months of residency, I became the assistant director of the center, and held that position for four years. During that time, I attended a Bible college in Seattle and received a bachelor's degree in theology. I graduated from the school and the drug rehabilitation center, and in January 1980, my wife, Wendy, and I started Christian Faith Center which I still pastor.

Since those days in the rehabilitation center, after four years of school and now ten years of pastoring, I have come to realize why so many Christians never walk in the peace, joy and freedom of their salvation. They try to break free from the hurts and hold of the world but never succeed. It is not that they have never been truly born again, or that they did not really "believe." For many, the problem is not in their spirits, but in their souls. Their minds have not been renewed. Though their spirits are recreated, their minds are not. The Word teaches us that our minds control our lives. To have God's perfect will, we must be transformed by the renewing of our minds. (Rom. 12:2.) Most Christians have either never been taught these truths or have not diligently applied them.

This book will help you to renew your mind and, more importantly, the spirit of your mind. It will help you create the kind of life that you desire and that God wants you to have. The principles you will learn through this book will cause you to prosper spiritually, mentally, physically, financially, and socially. Decide within yourself now to receive the truth that will make you free, and get ready to move into a more prosperous lifestyle.

FEED THE CHILDREN

LARRY JONES INTERNATIONAL MINISTRIES, INC.

Post Office Box 36, Oklahoma City, OK 73101-0036 • 405/942-0228 • Larry Jones, President

April 12, 1991

Mrs. Yukie S. Osumi
6721 17th Ave. NW
Seattle, WA 98117-5519

Dear Mrs. Osumi:

FOR
Roger

1

Renewing the Spirit of the Mind

This book can be an adventure in change for you.

This book addresses the source of most problems — the mind.

There may be many circumstances in your life that appear to be the source of all your problems. The way in which you deal with those circumstances is rooted in your mind.

If you try to change your attitudes or behavior without dealing with your basic mindset, the changes will only be temporary, and soon your mind will lead you into the same problems all over again. Once your mind has been renewed, you will discover your entire life changing for the better.

The first step in renewing your mind is to understand how the mind works, and see how it became the way it is now is. Your mind is a magnificent tool, and when you know how to use it, it will be a powerful tool to help you become what you want to be.

Your mind is the control mechanism of your entire life.

For as he thinketh in his heart, so is he.
Proverbs 23:7

When you change your thinking, you change your life. When your thinking becomes renewed, your whole life changes. That can happen in a negative *or* a positive way. When you change your thought processes in a positive way, you will begin to see positive changes in every aspect of your life. On the other hand, if you make negative changes, you will see negative changes overtake you in every aspect of your life.

"Programming" Starts Before Birth

Even before you were born, your mind was being "programmed." Most people do not realize this, and even many who do understand it, do not utilize the concept on a day-to-day basis. You have existing programs in your mental "computer" (brain) that control the way you get out of bed, the way you handle your job, and the way you respond to every activity each day of your life.

Most of the decisions you make are not conscious decisions, but are preconscious, preprogrammed, subconscious decisions.

Most of the fights we get into with our spouses are not started by a conscious choice. The fights start through a subconscious choice, a preprogrammed thought that causes us to respond to circumstances in a certain way.

So often we say, "I don't like these events. I don't like this relationship, I don't like these circumstances, or I don't like the way things are going." But we do not make changes because we do not realize that it first requires a subconscious change. The subconscious response must be "renovated" or renewed where the memory banks have filed away programmed behavior.

The Bible calls this programmed behavior the **spirit of your mind** (Eph. 4:23). The Apostle Paul wrote about this to a church at Ephesus almost two thousand years ago. He told the people of that church that each of them must renew the *spirit of his mind* in order to "put on" a new creation that was righteous, holy, and prosperous in every way.

Today we still need to put on a new creation. But I can tell you that it works! You can put on a new way of thinking. You can see a change in your life. As you renew your mind, and the spirit of your mind, that preprogrammed way of thinking will begin to change. The renewed mind then will bring about a different response in relationships, business, finances, and everything you do. When that happens, you will see new opportunities, and see other new positive results in your life. It really will make a difference in your life.

Those programmed thoughts stored away in your subconscious mind began to be filed even before you were born. It is a normal part of development to store information in "the spirit of the mind." As a child is developing in its mother's womb, it gathers data. Before the child is born it has collected data about the world it will enter. Is my world peaceful or is it troubled? Is my world happy, or is it sad? Is my world successful, or is it struggling?

As the child moves through childhood, additional programs are fed into the memory banks. The primary sources of input are parents, grandparents, baby sitters and so on. Their attitudes became your attitudes. Their lifestyle became your lifestyle. Even their gestures became your gestures. The spirits of their minds became part of the spirit of *your* mind. Your soul (mind, will, emotions) was shaped by their images.

11

My wife, Wendy, and I have three small children. We have seen our children reflect our image right before our eyes. Our attitudes, both positive and negative, have become part of them even before they were consciously aware of it.

Now this direct imprinting may be positive if your parents were prosperous, successful, fulfilled, healthy, and loving people. However, it can be negative if the people who programmed you were poor (literally or spiritually), or if they were failures, unhappy, sick, and unloving. If those "programmers" struggled through life and gave you the concept that "life is a struggle," your life can be miserable.

Over and over, it has been proven that as we grow up, we repeat the good and bad examples of our parents. As you know, the alcoholic parent very often produces alcoholic children. The abusive parent frequently produces abusive children, and the depressed parent produces depressed children.

The sins or the blessings of the parents are passed on to the third and the fourth generation. The good *and* the bad are passed on, the Bible says. (Num. 14:18.)

The Process Continues

As we began school and started going to church, other assumptions, beliefs, attitudes, and thoughts began to be fed into our minds. We adopted them without realizing what we were adopting. Friends and relatives both contributed to this process. As we moved through the later school years and finally entered the "real world," the environment we accepted has much to do with the preprogrammed spirit of our minds.

If you grew up in the South, you may have different attitudes toward home life than if you grew up in the North. If you grew up in Europe, the spirit of your mind will be very different than if you were raised in South America or North America.

Consciously, the attitudes and thoughts which you grew up with do not control your life, but subconsciously, they do. They control your life every day without you being aware of it.

For the first fifteen to twenty years of our lives, we put together this package of information called the *spirit of the mind*. It becomes our way of believing and our way of thinking. Sometime between fifteen and twenty years old, we conclude the gathering process and take what we have and go out to tackle life. We may continue in our education, and we may continue to gather technical data and other forms of information, but the spirit of our mind, the attitudes of our life, and the ways in which we generally approach life are usually established before we are twenty years old.

For the rest of our lives, we just live out those programs. We simply follow through with the things we learned subconsciously, and we do not change very much from that point on.

Of course, this pattern can be broken by people who sincerely *desire* change, who look for change, and who earnestly desire a new kind of lifestyle. You *can* renew your mind, and more importantly, you can renew the spirit of your mind.

However, this is not usually the case. Not many people change after their teen years. That is not to say you will not get a new job, or move to a new city, or change spouses or buy a new house, or change your appearance. There are many things you change as you go through life, but the spirit of your mind is usually not one of them.

Outward superficial things may change, but the real essence of your personality, attitudes and ways of handling things do not change very often after the teen years.

Changing the spirit of your mind takes an unusually great desire for *real* change. I believe as you read this book, you will become one of those people who seeks positive change.

Time-Release Beliefs

As you have been reading, has it occurred to you how many times *you* act without thinking? Somewhere in the past you were programmed to respond to certain situations in a particular way. Imagine what it would be like to approach each situation or circumstance without a preprogrammed response. By the time you finish reading this book, I believe you will be on your way to having a new approach to life.

Before discussing the mechanism of change, we need to look at one more type of programming, what I call *time-released beliefs*. These are programs that you do not realize are there until a specific incident brings them to the surface.

The older I get, the more I realize that my mind is filled with time-released beliefs. When I was younger, I did not really know what I believed about marriage or parenthood, or any other major adult issues.

However, when I later was married and began to raise children, ways of thinking began to pop out that I did not even know were part of my programming.

I will never forget the day my son, Caleb, was born. He was born at home. My wife and I and a few of our friends were there for the delivery. A couple of friends helped my wife, and I delivered the baby. Another friend made a video tape of the birth. When we played that tape later, I saw myself bathing and dressing our new son. When I heard myself talking to Caleb, Wendy and our friends, I was amazed, shocked really, to hear my father speaking. I saw his gestures, heard his tone and attitude when I talked to the baby! I realized there had been a time-released belief preprogrammed in the spirit of my mind. That particular situation caused those programmed behaviors to be released and I heard and saw myself doing things I never realized I would do.

As Caleb began to grow, he stopped being a cute little baby who did everything right and became a little boy who did some things wrong. I again saw attitudes in myself, and heard myself say the same words my father and mother had said to me when I was a little boy. I realized that although I had never thought those things, and had not consciously decided to do those things, a programmed response in me surfaced as I dealt with my little boy. And many times, I did not like what came out.

Perhaps you also remember your parents disciplining you in a certain way and saying, "I'll never treat *my* kids that way when I grow up and have kids." Yet there I was, doing the same things, carrying on the family tradition so to speak. I was going through the same routines my parents went through without consciously deciding to do them. The spirit of my mind, my attitudes, my beliefs, and my ways of thinking about raising children, was not being freely and objectively developed to fit the moment or the different personalities of my children. My actions reflected time-released programs stored in my memory banks years before.

Many people struggle with problems without realizing that they are not dealing with conscious decisions of today but rather they are responding with a way of thinking that has been hidden for years. The answer to overcoming problems is to renew the mind, to renew the way we think. You can go to psychologists or psychiatrists, and spend a lot of money trying to find out what Mom did or what Dad did, and why you continue to struggle. However, that cannot teach you how to renew the spirit of your mind.

You can go through hours and hours of therapy and still not see any change. Going back through the feelings, emotions, and circumstances of the past *will not change* a thing. You will not progress at all. You may discover *why* you have your problems, but you will still have the problems. You may know why you think the way you think, but you will still think the way you think!

What I want to show you is how to *change* those things that are keeping you from the life you want by renewing your mind and the spirit of your mind so those old beliefs, attitudes, and programs will no longer keep you from changing.

Learning Is Not Changing

In the same way that I saw myself acting as a parent similar to the way my own parents had acted, I began to realize that the way I made financial decisions was also a preprogrammed response. My decisions were not based on what would most likely bring financial success, but rather were based on attitudes toward money, possessions, and spending that I had adopted as I was growing up. Therefore, very often I found myself struggling financially because of the foolish things I did. I did not want to constantly struggle, but I continued to do foolish things until I renewed my mind about finances.

I see people every day in the same situation who are fed up with the way they are living. They do not like the way things are going, but they do not change. They have not found the key to change.

Another thing you need to understand is that *not everything* you do is patterned after what you saw growing up. Sometimes, we react *against* the things we saw in our early years and we act the opposite way. In this case, things you do today are exactly the opposite of what your parents did. However, your attitudes, beliefs, and behavior are *still programmed responses*. The spirit of your mind is simply programmed to respond opposite to your parents' behavior. Your life today is still being controlled by the past, although it is a reactionary control.

Another thing you must understand is that *learning is not changing.* Acquiring knowledge does not automatically renew your mind. More education or learning the psychological sociological circumstances of your past or present will not change your life. What I am talking about the Bible calls *renewal.*

In Romans, the Apostle Paul wrote:

> **And be not conformed to this world: but be ye transformed by the renewing of your mind, that ye may prove what is that good, and acceptable, and perfect, will of God.**
>
> **Romans 12:2**

The will of God is for you to live a prosperous, successful life. Spiritually, mentally, physically, financially, and socially, God desires prosperity for you. It is never His will for people to suffer or struggle through life. Suffering and struggling come when we are living contrary to His will for us.

You may think it is hard to live according to the will of God, but the Bible says it is hard to live the way of the transgressor. (Prov. 13:15.) Living in the will of God is the highest kind of life any man or woman will ever experience.

How do we get there? Paul said that to prove what the will of God is you must be transformed by the renewing of your mind. You must not be conformed to the world.

So, it seems obvious that the renewing of your mind will bring you into the perfect will of God. Education alone does not bring this highest kind of life. Well-educated people can be found among those whose lives evidence total failure. Living in a land of opportunity, many people still suffer and struggle, some even ending their lives in suicide. Many people with a good education suffer from drug and alcohol abuse. Learning can be an asset, but it is not the key to *real* change in your life.

A Caterpillar Is a Butterfly in Disguise

Look at the word *transformed* in Romans 12:2. Literally, it means metamorphosis, a complete change in form. What Paul was saying was that if the people in the church at Rome were willing to be changed, they could have the highest kind of life. And if that was true for them, it is still true for us today.

A caterpillar may look up at a butterfly flying through the air and say, "Man, he's got it made in the shade!" He may say, "I have to live on this twig and barely crawl along. My whole world is wrapped up in this little branch. I have to eat these funny little leaves, and the best I can do is get a new branch with new leaves. But that guy is flying!"

He watches the butterfly go by overhead, bright, colorful, and free, flying everywhere experiencing a very exciting life. Now the caterpillar can also have this same life, if he is willing to go through a metamorphosis. You know how the process works: The caterpillar spins a cocoon, puts himself in an uncomfortable circumstance for a while, and then through the process of time, he is changed completely. He becomes totally different. He is transformed and leaves his cocoon as a butterfly.

It is exciting to think of spreading your wings with a whole new outlook on life, entering into a whole new realm. It is exciting to have something new and bright, something you only could dream of in the past. But to get there, you must go through a metamorphosis.

How do you do that? Paul said it was by the **renewing of your mind.** *Renewing* means to change or exchange. *To renew* does not mean to learn more, to educate, or to add to. It means to change or exchange.

If someone who was working for me continued to be unproductive in spite of the fact that I did everything I could do to bring change into his life, I might have to *exchange* him for someone else. I might have to put someone else into that position to get the job done the way it should be done.

In the same way, if your way of thinking has not brought the results you want, after you tried learning more, reading more, taking more seminars, or even getting another job, then you must *make an exchange* in your mind, the control center of your life.

The **good, acceptable, and perfect, will of God** makes the highest kind of spiritual, mental, physical, financial, and social success possible.

When does that come? When you are transformed.

How do you get transformed? By renewing your mind.

What is *renewing* the mind? It is taking out the old thoughts and old attitudes, removing the old spirit of the mind, and gaining a new way of thinking. It is not just gaining new thoughts but gaining *a new way* of thinking. This does not mean just getting new ideas but rather getting *a new spirit* of the mind. When this happens, you will enter into a new life.

Why People Resist Change

Many people resist change because they have tried to change but failed, and do not want to fail again. How many times have you tried to change? Well, now you know that wanting to change is not enough. You must be completely *transformed*. A mental *exchange* needs to take place. You must remove some things from your thinking and replace them with new programs. If you know how, change is not all that difficult.

If you resist change because you think people around you are controlling you, or trying to change you, then you *really* need to renew your mind. You have *really* missed it. You are millions of miles from the source of your problem. You have your finger pointed at everyone else, instead of yourself. You have put the blame on other people, who really have no control over your thinking, and have neglected the one who does — you.

Your life is not at the mercy of everyone else. Yes, other people can affect you and they can have a certain amount of influence over you. But *you* decide how that influence will affect you. You decide if a mountain is a platform to blast off from to reach great heights, or a wall that will stop you in your tracks.

You decide if difficulties will make you stronger so you can overcome problems easily, or if they will defeat you and keep you from moving ahead.

You are in control of the renewing of your mind. You really can make your life whatever you want it to be. But as long as you point the finger at others, you will never change, you will never grow, and your life will be stagnant until you die.

To renew or to exchange your mind is a lot like changing a baby's diaper. As a father of young children, I can relate to this image. I have changed many diapers!

When your children need their diapers changed, they begin to fuss because they are uncomfortable. Then they begin to smell, and the odor makes everyone else uncomfortable! So what do you do? A wise parent grabs the baby, sprinkles a little powder on him and puts on a clean diaper.

But wait a minute! I left out a very important step. You take off the dirty diaper first.

Many of us are going through life with stinking thinking, and we need "changing" really badly. Our "diaper" — the state of our minds — is causing our whole life to stink. We need changing, but all we do is sprinkle a little powder on top and try to cover up with a clean diaper over the old one.

But this does not solve the problem. Very soon, the "odor" can be detected again. To eliminate the problem and exchange a dirty diaper for a clean one, there is a proper procedure to follow.

First, you remove the old diaper and clean up the baby.

Then, when the baby is clean and fresh, you put on the new diaper. Then the baby is comfortable, and no longer makes others uncomfortable. All is well.

And so it is with renewing the mind and the spirit of the mind. If you do not remove old programmed thoughts, but merely try to add on to your old way of thinking, you are not going to change very much. This is why many people never make lasting changes in their lives. They just continue adding on to the same old way of thinking.

Look at what frequently happens with divorce and remarriage. Nine times out of ten, the second marriage is no better than the first. The only difference is the name of the spouse you fight with. Why? Because when you marry the second time, you bring the same person into that marriage you brought into the first one.

What happens when you change jobs because you had problems with the last one? Usually, there is not much improvement. You might make a little more money and even be able to buy a nicer car or house. But the person who was part of the problem in the first job is the same person operating in the second job — you. Eventually, you feel the same way about your new job. You go through the same kind of problems, struggle with the same difficulties, and basically continue in the same direction.

Changing the outward circumstance does not affect your life very much. "Adding to" does not change your life in any real way. What works is taking off the old and replacing it with the new.

If you change the inside, the outside will take care of itself. When you plant the proper seed in your mind, you are going to find the fruit that you are looking for.

In Matthew, Jesus said:

> **A good man out of the good treasure of the heart bringeth forth good things: and an evil man out of the evil treasure bringeth forth evil things.**
> **Matthew 12:35**

Look at what Jesus is saying in this verse. Out of your heart (mind), you will bring forth good things or evil things.

What decides what you bring forth? Heredity, good luck, or the environment in which you live? No, what determines what comes out of you is simply *what is already in you.* Your life is a manifestation of what is in you. Your marriage is a manifestation of what is in you concerning marriage. Your children are a manifestation of what is in you concerning children. Your finances are a manifestation of what is in you concerning finances. Your business or job is a manifestation of what is in you concerning work.

If you are not experiencing the things you want, do not keep working on the outside! Start working on the treasure that is inside you, because when you change the "treasure," you will change what is brought forth.

As an illustration, I am sure you have heard of new apartment projects being built for people from the "slums." Within a year, the beautiful new housing development is run-down, filthy, and in the same poverty-stricken condition that the people came from. Why? Because the preprogrammed thinking the people had about their living condition was not exchanged for new thinking.

The external is always a manifestation of the internal. If we try to impose external changes, our internal programmed thinking will cause us to do whatever is necessary to bring things "back to normal," back to fit whatever subconscious program is directing in that area of life. We will lose it, destroy it, "blow it," or whatever is necessary to "get back to normal."

Some time ago a study was done in Canada on a group of one hundred lottery winners. These were people who had won more than a million dollars. This study took place over a period of more than twenty years. More than 90 percent of those lottery winners had nothing to show for their winnings after about twenty years. They were back to their "normal" existence before they had won the lottery.

It is only when you change internally that you see a sustained change externally. If you do not change inside, no matter what happens, sooner or later, you will get back to what is "normal" for you.

By now, I am sure you are wondering, "What exactly is programmed in my mind? How did it get there, and how can I deal with it?"

I believe you must be courageous and discover those areas of preprogrammed response that are holding you back. Whatever you have to deal with is worth it to get good treasure built up in your mind, so that you can experience the perfect will of God for your life.

In the next chapter, we will examine the treasure in your heart and count up your mental "net worth."

2
What Is Your Mental Net Worth?

In the financial world, an accounting process reveals what your assets are and what your liabilities are. The assets and liabilities are added together to show whether you are in a positive or negative situation. The bottom line is the net worth.

In this chapter, I want you to take stock of your mental inventory and find your balance between assets and liabilities. If the assets outweigh the liabilities, you are experiencing a happy and productive life. If not, then most likely, you are experiencing many problem areas in your life.

You need to know what is being fed into your memory bank. If it is good treasure, it will bring you great returns. If it is not good treasure, then what you are storing up will bring destruction.

I also want to give you five practical steps to ensure that you are building a positive future.

When Your Mind Changes, Your Life Changes

Renewing your mind involves changes in your conscious thinking, but what are more important are changes in the spirit of your mind. Important changes in your life are manifestations of the inward changes you have made.

It is not the outward things I want you to focus on — it is the inward things. Often, people are so concerned with changing outward things that all their time is spent dealing with them, and they never get to the true root of change. Consequently, in spite of all the time spent, very few things ever really change.

In the first chapter, we saw that our minds are the controlling mechanisms of our lives. Your mind is a computer that stores information and controls the way things happen. It controls decisions and choices. In your family, business, finances, health, and all you do, your mind is the controlling mechanism. To the degree that your mind is renewed, you will begin to experience change, and you will enter into a renewed life.

If you continue to focus on the outward things, you will miss the changes that are possible. The aches, sniffles, and fever that go with a cold are not the cold, they are the symptoms of it. They are not the problem, but a manifestation of the problem. You can deal with the symptoms but still have the cold.

Most of us deal with life's symptoms. We focus on outward things and look at circumstances. Because we spend our time focused on the symptoms, we do not get to the root cause of the problem.

Whatever is stored in you is either good or bad treasure, and that is what you bring forth each day. Perhaps your stored treasure is partly good and partly bad. You may not have an "evil" treasure inside you, but you may have a mediocre treasure.

I believe Christians today are tired of mediocrity. However, being tired of it does not mean you know how to change it. Being tired of where you are is simply an expression of your frustration. But being tired and frustrated will not produce any changes.

When you begin to change the spirit of your mind, you begin to change the kind of treasure that is within you. Your mind is not the totality of that treasure, it is only one part of it. However, it *is* a major part and the key to changing all of the treasure.

Jesus said your heart contains the treasure, and your heart is the place where your soul and spirit meet.

Your "treasure" is made up of thoughts, beliefs, assumptions, and doctrines that you accept as true. Your treasure is what you base your decisions and attitudes on, and it can bring success or it can bring failure.

In other words, your treasure is what you live on. All you do every day of your life comes out of that treasure. It is a "bank account" for life. You draw on that bank account and bring out currency to deal with your spouse. You make a withdrawal every time you are with friends and neighbors. You make a withdrawal when you interact with other people on your job or at your business.

Every day, all of us make withdrawals from the treasure in our hearts. If your treasure is negative, a withdrawal may bring the currency of worry, strife, or contention. Then you end up trying to "pay" your way through life with fear, depression, and resentment.

If things around you are negative, then that is a reflection of what you have stored away in your heart. If you are struggling financially, your treasure is a poverty mentality. If you are continually experiencing sickness and disease, then you have that treasure in your heart. Therefore, every day you bring that forth you experience physical problems.

Your Treasure Is Reflected as Symptoms

If you have been divorced or are having problems in your marriage, you or your spouse have a treasure stored up that is contrary to a successful marriage.

It is easy to spot the things in your treasure that need changing by looking at the negative symptoms you see in your life. It is also easy to spot your good treasure from the successful, fruitful manifestations that show up in your life everyday.

You can see what is inside you by what is coming out of you. Every problem in your life is like a printed page from your mind, held up for all to read. We *live out* our thinking. The importance of understanding this is not so you can figure out what is wrong with everyone else, but so you can look at yourself and see where you need to improve.

This valuable truth is a puzzle to many people, but the Holy Spirit gave it to us very plainly in Scripture.

> **And he called the multitude, and said unto them, Hear, and understand:**
>
> **Not that which goeth into the mouth defileth a man; but that which cometh out of the mouth, this defileth a man.**
>
> **Then came his disciples, and said unto him, Knowest thou that the Pharisees were offended, after they heard this saying?**
>
> **But he answered and said, Every plant, which my heavenly Father hath not planted, shall be rooted up.**

> **Let them alone: they be blind leaders of the blind. And if the blind lead the blind, both shall fall into the ditch.**
>
> **Then answered Peter and said unto him, Declare unto us this parable.**
>
> **And Jesus said, Are ye also yet without understanding?**
>
> **Do not ye yet understand, that whatsoever entereth in at the mouth goeth into the belly, and is cast out into the draught?**
>
> **But those things which proceed out of the mouth come forth from the heart; and they defile the man.**
> **Matthew 15:10-18**

In the verse following these, Jesus went on to list the kinds of things that come from the heart. The first thing he mentioned was *evil thoughts*. After that He listed murder, adultery, theft, giving false witness, and blasphemy. He said *those* are the things that defile you, not the outward things.

Jesus was teaching His disciples important principles, and through the Word He continues teaching *us* that what we think comes out in our behavior and our lifestyle.

A homosexual person may say, "I was born this way. This is natural for me." No, God made man, and God made woman, but God did not make a man in a woman's body nor a woman in a man's body. God does not make mistakes such as that. God made Adam and Eve, not Adam and Steve.

A person is a homosexual because he, or she, began to think "maybe I am that way. I need to explore all the possibilities." The first little thought was a seed

31

that multiplied into a great negative harvest. The seed might also have been an emotional problem relating to the opposite sex brought about by a bad relationship with a mother or father. Those thoughts and emotions then produced their negative, destructive homosexual lifestyle.

Every Action Begins With a Thought

Jesus said even murder begins with a thought. So where do financial dilemmas come from? Where do emotional dilemmas come from? Out of the thoughts of the heart.

What I want you to see is that you can *change* the treasure of your heart. Once you change that treasure, you can begin to make positive withdrawals. Instead of bringing forth things that cause problems, you can bring forth new things that will end your problems.

When your mind is renewed, you can bring forth love and peace. You can bring forth forgiveness and patience and all of the other positive things of life. When your mind is negative, you bring forth disagreement, fighting, and bitterness. You bring forth anger and depression, and other negative things of life.

Remember! Those negative things do not just fall on you. Bitterness, anger, and depression do not come on you from outside. They are not little clouds that float around the country and every once in a while, let down their rain on you.

People use the old saying, "I got up on the wrong side of the bed," to excuse the bad things coming out of the negative treasure in their hearts. But the side of the bed you get up on has nothing to do with the fruit in your life.

Others may say, "Well, I'm just in a bad mood." No, it is not a "mood"; it is a way of thinking. Someone else would say, "I must be under a dark cloud today." That also is just a way of thinking.

When your way of thinking changes, all of life changes. You *choose* what goes on in your life. You choose how far you will go. In the Old Testament, this principle is described in a very strong way:

> **I call heaven and earth to record this day against you, that, I have set before you life and death, blessing and cursing: therefore choose life, that both thou and thy seed may live.**
> **Deuteronomy 30:19**

This is a powerful choice. Life and death, blessings or cursings are set before you to choose. Which one do you want? Which will you choose? The choice is not up to your family, the government, or your company. It is not even up to your spouse. *You* choose life or death. The choices you have made already have built your treasure, and what you are experiencing is the consequence of what you think and believe. You control what you choose. But then, what you choose controls you. So choose carefully!

Cycles of Life

Many times, when I counsel couples having marital problems, one of them will say, "I really believe that if I would leave my spouse, my life would be a lot better." I talk with the couple about how they can improve their marriage, and how they can resolve their differences and problems. But when they come back a week later, one of them will say: "Well, I tried to do what you said, but I still am thinking about divorce. If I could get away, it would be different, and everything would be better."

When I ask how often they have tried to solve things by leaving, many times they answer, "This is my second marriage," or "my third," or, "I have left several times and come back."

In other words, they have created a way of thinking that says, "If I can get out of this marriage and find someone new, something different, my life will be better."

I tell them that this marriage is no better than their first (or second) one. *They* are still the same person. Their problem has nothing to do with their spouse. They are the problem. But they continue holding on to the belief that if they change spouses, they would have a better life, even though changing spouses last time did not make life better.

When you accept the thought that outward things must change before you can feel differently, you are locked into a never-ending cycle. You have become a lifetime "runner." You run from relationships, from responsibilities, and from change.

You will end up running from the very thing that can make a difference in your life — that is, the renewing of your mind. If you stop running, break the habit of rebelling against God's way of changing, and choose a new way of thinking, your life will change.

A wise person once said, "Everywhere you go, there *you* are." That may sound simple, but it is really profound. You may try to run, but you have to take yourself along wherever you go. If you have wrong thoughts, it creates bad situations. You may try to find escape by running from yourself, but the thing that really made the situation bad was what was in your mind. And bad thinking goes along with you to the next situation,

By renewing the spirit of your mind, you can break this cycle. Stretch yourself to change your thinking so that your problems will not be repeated over and over.

Five Steps to Change

I want to give you five steps that will bring change to every realm of your life. These steps will work in marriage, finances, physical health, and raising children. These steps will bring lasting change. Later I will deal with specific topics, but at this point I want to give you the basic principles.

The first step is to take *responsibility*. Take full responsibility for yourself and your life. Do not blame God. Do not blame your spouse. Do not blame your neighbor or your boss. Take full responsibility. If you do not, nothing else will help you. If you do not accept complete responsibility for the condition of your life, nothing will work. Until you take full responsibility, you remain out of control, incapable of change. You will be sentenced to a life of maintenance, running like mad just to stay in the same place. *Take full responsibility.*

The second step is to *rethink*. Rethink what you believe and what you assume is true. Rethink what you believe is right and what you assume is the way to handle life. Rethink your concepts for living and what you base your decisions on. If you do not begin to rethink some of your concepts, you could be living by concepts that are totally wrong. *Rethink what you think.*

The third step is to *reject*. Reject your old ways. Reject the old thoughts that come back to you and block your ability to change. This is one of the most difficult steps, because the old habits of thinking are hard to break. Many times, when I said I was going to change and think a new way, I found myself slipping back into the old way again.

Let me give you a practical example. My wife, Wendy, and I have discussed this behavior many times. She will say to me, "You do not talk to me enough about your feelings and share your thoughts with me. You pick up a magazine or turn on the television instead of talking to me, and that makes me feel unimportant."

So I say to myself, "I'm going to change this pattern and begin to communicate and share with my wife. I am not going to pick up a magazine or a book. I will just relax and share with her."

I *really* want to do it. I know this is the right decision. I think about it, and decide to start a new way of thinking. Then the next thing I know, I am right back in the same old way. I go through the same old habits and patterns, my wife is frustrated again and I hear her say, "You always do that! You always pick up a magazine, or you turn on the television. Why don't you change?"

I *want* to change, and I have decided to change, but here I am, doing the same thing again. I know you can relate to this kind of pattern when it comes to losing weight, or managing money, or communicating with your spouse. There are many behavior patterns we all have in common.

What I have to do is reject my old way of thinking every time it comes back, When the thought comes to me to pick up a magazine or do something by myself, I must reject it *before* I follow through with the action. To break that habit of acting without thinking, I must be alert to catch that triggering thought and push it out of my mind.

I must consciously take hold of that thought and say, "No! This is a negative thought. I do not want to do this, and I am not *going* to do it." This stops the cycle before it continues into action.

Letting negative thoughts run into action, then repenting and making a resolution not to do it again will not break a negative cycle. The way to break it is to catch it when it starts to run and stop it. After a few times, the cycle will be broken. But you must reject the cycle right on the spot, right then while it is trying to repeat itself. Do not go through the old routine again. *Reject that old way of thinking.*

Step number four is to *review*. Review the new thoughts. Meditate on your new way of thinking. Practice thinking these new thoughts. When you are driving your car, instead of "spacing out" on some ungodly, depressed, radio personality, practice your new way of thinking. Instead of wasting your mental time, practice your new way of thinking.

In the example I gave you about changing the way I communicate with my wife, I began to practice a new way of thinking when I was driving, when I was eating lunch, and when I was in my office alone. I would practice these thoughts. "I just love to talk with Wendy. I enjoy communicating and sharing with her. It is good to have a lovely wife I can sit and talk with and share myself with, and tell her how I think and how I feel. I really enjoy it."

Now, in the past, I did not enjoy it because I was being turned inward, and locked into the habit of not sharing. But when I began to renew my way of thinking, I learned to enjoy communicating with my wife.

You have to review and practice a new way of thinking, or it will never become a part of you. Go over it, and over it, and over it. You can call it meditation, or you can call it practicing. But it really is reviewing your new thoughts.

Suppose you have a problem with money. Perhaps you consistently spend all of your money before you earn it. Your credit cards are charged to the limit, so you get another one and charge it to the limit, too! Perhaps you are barely getting by and are behind in your payments. You really need to practice a new way of thinking. You need to review new thoughts about handling money. Instead of watching television, begin reviewing a new way of thinking.

Think, "I enjoy living debt free. It feels good to pay for things when I buy them, not six months or a year later. It is nice to have money in the bank and have all my bills paid. I am disciplined with my money. I only spend money I have after I have paid my bills and have saved some money to invest in my future. I am in control of my finances."

Now, as you review these new thoughts, you are practicing a new way to think about money. So, when you get into a store and see something you really cannot afford, you will have a new way of thinking that says, "No, I am not going to buy that because I am a good money manager. I am disciplined in my spending. I invest my money. I save my money. I do not 'blow' my money."

By reviewing these new thoughts, you strengthen your new lifestyle and bring change into your life.

The fifth step is to *resound*. This means to speak your new thoughts so they "resound" out loud. Just like reviewing, which was talking to yourself, you also have to speak your thoughts out loud. I have found that if you do not speak out your new way of thinking, it will never become a new way of thinking, which means you will never change anything in your life. You have to speak your new thoughts out loud.

Perhaps your wife has confronted you about spending more time together as a family, and you respond with, "Well, I bring home money for you. Isn't that good enough?" No, it is not! Your wife wants *you* more than she wants money. In order to change, you must allow the new thoughts to *resound* from your mouth.

You might start saying things like, "I love spending time with my wife. I love communicating and sharing with my wife. I love to go home and spend an evening with my family."

Maybe if your problem is money, you constantly say, "Everytime I get any money, it just seems to slip through my fingers. It just disappears. I don't know where all the money goes. I can't hang onto money; I must have holes in my pocket. Someone must be stealing from my bank account. I have never been able to save money."

As long as you speak out the problem, and repeat what is wrong, you will continue with more of what is wrong. But when you begin to say something new and start saying the way you want life to be, you will have what you want.

So the last key to renewing your mind is "resounding" the new thoughts in your mind by speaking your new way of thinking.

A Summary of the Five Steps

It is important for you to have a solid grip on these five principles, so I will review them quickly.

Number one is to be *responsible*. Many people avoid taking responsibility so that they have no control over their situations. Without control, you cannot change anything. However, the truth is that you *are* in control. And the responsibility to change is yours.

Number two is *to rethink*. Challenge what you believe, what you assume to be true, and what you have been told. If these are not working, give new thoughts a chance to prove themselves.

Number three is *to reject the old way*. If your old thoughts have produced the problems you have today, make room for their replacement by rejecting your old thoughts.

Number four is *to review the new*. You need to capture new thoughts, but going over them once is not enough. In order to have them work, you need to imprint them deeply in your mind by reviewing and practicing your new thinking over and over again.

Number five is *to resound* your new thoughts. This means to speak them. Repeat new thoughts to yourself, and speak them to your family and friends. This is the secret ingredient that will create permanent change in you. Speaking thoughts out loud will lock them permanently in your mind, and positive results will surely follow.

Now let us continue this exciting adventure into your new way of life.

If you do these five "R's" — responsibility, rethinking, rejecting, reviewing, and resounding — you will start the process of change. You will bring new things in your life. What will happen is that you will change your treasure. Then, you will have something new to draw from. You will have something that will make a difference in your life.

Many people are waiting for their ship to come in, but if their ship did come in, their thinking would sink it in the harbor! It is not a matter of waiting for something outside of you, but it is a matter of changing something inside of you.

There is one last thought I want to share in this chapter taken from Third John 2: You will **prosper and be in health, even as thy soul prospers.**

A prosperous soul is what I hope this book will help you possess. A *prosperous soul* has an abundance of peace, joy, and prosperity in every realm of life. These things must be *in* you before they can be *around* you. They have to come out of your heart. A prosperous soul is the beginning of a prosperous life.

Living in a prosperous country does not guarantee that you will be prosperous. We see people in the richest country in the world living on the streets without a place to sleep. They live on sidewalks and sleep in parks, or they live in run-down, filthy places. Yet they live in a nation with more opportunities to prosper than you can imagine.

The other day, I saw a man with a big sign that said, "No job, no food, no money. Please help!" He had a bucket in front of him, and he wanted people to put money in it. As I drove past him, I thought, "Boy, that is sad. What a tragedy. I feel for that man."

He was standing there, holding his sign, waving at all the cars going past. Yet within a mile, I passed four businesses with "Help Wanted" signs. Four of them! Instead of standing there waiting for someone to come and change his circumstances for him, he could have changed his own circumstances.

This does not mean I do not have compassion for him or other poor people. But the fact remains, if we took all the money in the world and dispersed it evenly to every person, there is enough wealth in our world for everyone to have approximately twelve million dollars. This includes everyone in China, India, and Africa, every man, woman, and child on the planet Earth.

However, if we disposed all the wealth today, within five years, all of it would be back in the same hands again, and most of those who are poor today would be poor again. It is what is in us that controls what is coming out of us. Our thoughts, beliefs, and attitudes control our lives.

There is no fountain of youth. There is no "get-quick-rich" scheme. No one is going to change everything around you and make your life better. You can prosper outwardly when you begin to prosper inwardly. By renewing the spirit of your mind, you can begin to change your life.

Out of the good treasure of your heart, you will bring forth a great life. Out of the negative treasure of your heart, you will continue to bring forth a negative life.

Look at your circumstances, and you will see whether the liabilities of your negative thoughts outweigh the assets of your good thoughts. If your heart is "running in the red," begin to make entries on the positive side and eliminate entries on the negative side until you have a positive balance in the treasure of your heart.

3
Finding Your Mental "Roots"

Have you ever told anyone, "I have already made up my mind?" I think all of us have made this statement or others like it to demonstrate that we are capable of making an independent decision. However, our "independent" decision is often made based on old information programmed in our minds. We simply retrieve old information from our subconscious minds and deliver it in the form of a "decision."

So what happens if you have false information stored away? Not even being aware of it, you will use it to make wrong decisions. You need to learn how to discover those areas of your thinking that lead to bad decisions. It is not difficult to change those thought patterns, but it may not happen immediately. Changing your thinking does take time, and requires using the five steps I outlined in the last chapter.

You *can* change any part of your life: physical, mental, spiritual, financial, and social. Any area of your life can be changed. *The key is changing your mind and your way of thinking.* You decide what you will think, and then your thinking determines what will happen in your life. So choose your thoughts carefully!

The Key to Change

In this chapter, we are going to explore the area of the subconscious. The subconscious mind is discussed quite a bit by psychologists and psychiatrists who work with behavioral change. They deal with some truth; however, psychiatry is the world's interpretation of God's "psychology." God's "psychology" is revealed in scriptures that show us how man's soul is related to the body and spirit.

Your subconscious mind must be changed in order for your life to change. Ways of thinking that were learned when you grew up are still affecting many decisions in your life. The exciting thing is that you can change what has been stored in your subconscious, which in turn will change the choices and decisions you make.

Many of your decisions were actually preprogrammed years ago. Many of your decisions about marriage were made when you were a teenager. Many of your decisions about friendship and relationships were made years ago by things you experienced or learned in some other way.

By the time you reached your early teen years, your decisions about marriage, handling money, and working were already formed. Now you are living out that programmed way of thinking.

I have worked with many people in prisons. If you talk to the average prisoner in a state penitentiary, county jail, or city jail, you will not find many inmates who enjoy living behind bars. It is extremely rare to find someone who is happier locked up. A majority of prisoners want to get out, yet most of them who get out will be back again.

You may say, "If they do not like prison, why do they live the kind of life that will ensure their return?"

The reason is that their subconscious minds are programmed with antisocial thinking so that they automatically move back into that kind of life and get caught again and are returned to prison.

They will tell you, "I don't like this way of living; it's terrible." Yet most of them will never change. They will continue to approach life the same way and have the same problems year after year after year.

We see this same kind of example on a daily basis. Certain individuals or families have continual financial problems. They barely get by and barely make ends meet. If they had a raise of $500 a month in income, within the month, that money would also be spent, and they would be in the same situation.

Most people believe that if they had more money, they would live better and be better off. Yet when they do make more, they often get into more financial bondage and have more debt to struggle with. This is not to say that you should not make more money. I believe you should. However, the key to prosperity is not to make more money, but to renew your mind so that when you do make more money, you will be able to manage it properly.

What do you really want out of life? Do you find yourself moving farther and farther away from what you want in spite of everything you do? Is there some hidden programmed thinking preventing you from success and fulfillment? Let's look into your thinking process and find out how to make it produce what you really want.

Reflex Thinking

I want to share some keys that will enable you to change your subconscious processes, the spirit of your mind, so that you can make choices that line up with the Word of God. I want you to avoid going through the same difficulties over and over again.

First, I want you to think about this term: *reflex thoughts*. Most people understand they have muscles in their bodies that were created to react to stimuli without any conscious thought. Your lungs are part of a reflex system or an automatic reaction system. You do not have to think about breathing or tell yourself to breath. Your heart is also a reflex organ. It pumps blood through your body without you thinking about it. As you read this book, you are not thinking about keeping your heart going. The heart does its work automatically.

If you hit your leg right below the kneecap, you will see a muscle react automatically. Your leg will jump without you telling it to. As a matter of fact, it will react even if you try to stop it!

You have thoughts that operate just like that. All of the thoughts that are in your subconscious are *reflex thoughts*. Those thoughts are the ones that automatically trigger certain words, behavior, and patterns in your life. They are thoughts you are not thinking for the first time.

Unfortunately most of our lives are spent reacting to the *reflex thoughts* in our subconscious. We may think we are in charge of our lives, but in reality we are not. We think we are making independent decisions, but in reality, we are making reflex decisions.

There are thinking habits, just as there are physical habits that must be broken. In today's world, no one thinks smoking tobacco is beneficial. I doubt if there are any people who still think smoking is harmless! Yet many people still smoke! The health hazards of smoking, the expense, and the unpleasantness of the smoke have been part of smoking since the first tobacco was taken back to England.

However, it took the national campaign linking smoking with an increased risk of cancer to cause many people to change the program in their subconscious mind that said, "Smoking is harmless. Smoking actually is pleasant. I *have* to smoke, and no one is going to make me quit if I don't want to!" Even then, because of the fight against the physical addiction, after the thought program was changed, many people have not been able to change this particular reflex.

Most smokers do not think about lighting the first cigarette they smoke in the morning. They just get up, automatically grab a cigarette and light it without ever making a conscious decision to do so. That is called "a habit." They never think about getting a cigarette out of the pack or lighting the match, or sucking the smoke into their lungs and blowing it out. Those things have become reflex actions.

There are so many examples like this in our everyday lives: drinking coffee, driving to and from work, washing the dishes, and so forth. After a few times of doing something the same way, we tend to file that thing away as a "program," and from then on, we do that particular thing without ever thinking about it.

How do we do this? These things become "habits" because of the subconscious part of our minds. When God created the subconscious mind, it was good. It was designed to allow the conscious part of our minds to remain free to analyze new data. But, programmed with the world's negative thinking, our subconscious minds can become a liability instead of an asset.

Renew the Spirit of the Mind

You can be a positive person, and yet have a negative "spirit of the mind." Again, let me say, I am using the term "spirit" in the abstract sense of attitudes and ways of thinking. For example, the *Spirit of America* is what we call "Americanism," a way of thinking that is peculiar to the people of this country.

I sometimes call the subconscious part of the mind "the robot mind," because it is totally programmed to trigger actions reflexively. Your subconscious mind does not think. It only reacts according to preprogrammed information. The *spirit of the mind* is the overall attitude you have toward life, made up of all of the separate little programs you learned by your teen years.

If those attitudes have been basically negative, then you have a negative mindset. You tend to see the worst in everything and in everyone. We call people like this pessimists. Others seemingly see through rose-colored glasses and are just as unrealistic. We call those people optimists. Most of us fall somewhere in the middle of these two extremes. We are optimistic about some things and pessimistic about other things.

So, in order to change, you must realize that you do have *a spirit of your mind,* a certain overall way of thinking. I am not talking about spiritual matters or a "mystical" sort of thing; I am talking about the very practical, everyday mechanics of the way your mind works.

If you do not change the *spirit of your mind,* the present mechanics of your mind will continue to operate just as they were programmed to years ago. No matter how many books you read or sermons you hear, you will still be the same. No matter how hard you try to change, you will be the same until the *spirit of your mind* is renewed to the image of Christ.

Changing the Mindsets of the Israelites

Remember how the nation of Israel was set free from Egypt and the bondage of Pharoah? Supernaturally led by God, they crossed the Red Sea and walked through the wilderness headed for the Promised Land. Oh, what exciting days those were! They were no longer slaves. They no longer had to make bricks for the Egyptians. They no longer had to eat leaks, garlic, and live off the flesh-pots. They were delivered and set free. Now they could have the life they had dreamed about. God was working on their behalf.

But as they headed toward the Promised Land, they began to run into problems. First, there was no water. Rather than thinking that God could provide water, they said:

"We want to go back to Egypt. We are going back to our old lifestyle. We would rather be slaves than be out here in this wilderness."

God did provide water, but the spirit of their minds did not change. A few days later, they ran into another problem. God provided fresh food every day, yet they began to murmur again. They wanted meat. So God flew in all the meat they could eat until most of them could not stand any more.

Several different times during those first two years in the wilderness, they ran into difficulties — and they murmured against God. Each time, they had a "programmed" thought, an operative phrase that came out of their mouths. It was, "Would God we had stayed in Egypt."

That phrase gives us a clue as to the state of their minds. They had lived in Egypt for four hundred years. The customs, fashions, and culture of that country had become theirs. They had lived in bondage for the last part of that period. Nevertheless, the Israelites who were led out by Moses had been slaves all of their lives. Their fathers, and probably their grandfathers, had also been slaves. They had a "slave" mentality, a *state of mind* that caused them to feel uncomfortable with freedom and caused them to expect to be provided for. The spirit of their mind was negative. They were used to grumbling and complaining. So, although God had promised them many good things, led them by a pillar of fire by day and a cloud by night, and gave them food and water, the only way they were able to handle difficulties was to grumble and murmur against the One in authority.

They finally got to the border of the Promised Land in spite of their rebellion and disobedience. There they looked over into the land of Canaan, the land which flowed with milk and honey. When the twelve spies returned from their reconnaissance mission into Canaan, it is apparent that only two of them had allowed God's dealings with them in the wilderness to *renew the spirit of their minds.* The two, of course, were Caleb and Joshua. They were the only two spies who saw the land clearly but could still believe God would continue to do in the future what He had done for them over the past two years.

The other spies grumbled and complained, "There are giants over there. They are too big for us, too powerful. We will never be able to inhabit the land. Moses has brought us out here just to destroy us. This is too hard. Let's go back to Egypt."

We are appalled when we read this account in the 13th and 14th chapters of the book of Numbers. Yet we operate the same way today as the Israelites did then and for the same reason. We do not renew the spirit of our minds.

Their thinking controlled their behavior, and they got exactly what their minds were programmed for — defeat and destruction. Was it God's will for them to waste their lives in the wilderness? Was it His will for a delay of another thirty-eight years before the Israelites occupied the Promised Land? No, but as they thought in their hearts, so they were. (Prov. 23:7.)

God could get the people out of Egypt, but He could not get Egypt out of the people. The spirit of their minds defeated them. God could deliver them from Egyptian bondage, but He could not deliver them from the bondage of their minds. Why? Is He not all-powerful, all-knowing, and omnipresent? Yes, He is, but He will not override the freedom of choice that He created in man. If He did, He would be forcing His will and His choice on us. God abides by His own principles, and the terms and limits for man that He established.

God solved this situation with a very interesting answer. He told them that everyone who was twenty years old and younger would enter the Promised Land. Everyone older than twenty would die in the wilderness except for Caleb and Joshua, who would become their new leaders.

Apparently, once you reach twenty, you tend to have your mind set in such a way that it becomes very, very difficult to change. Most people will *not* change. They would rather die than admit they need to change. So, most people do not change after twenty.

Younger people have it much easier. They are more open to change, and it is easier to renew the spirit of their minds. There seems to be a point, after a pattern has been repeated over and over, that our thinking becomes almost set in concrete. After a certain way of thinking is established long enough, it becomes a "stronghold," an area of your mind, fortified by custom, set against change. Any change, then, appears to be a threat, and your self-defense mechanisms go into operation against change to protect the status quo.

However, it is important to remember that *there is no limitation set by God against change after a certain age.* You do not have to accept the old adage about not being able to teach old dogs new tricks. It *is* possible to change thought patterns at any age. The "lever" to pry out the old and replace it with new, is *to want to change it badly enough.*

My question to you is this: Do you want to renew the spirit of your mind, or would you rather hang onto the old? Do you want to go into a new, abundant, promised land, or would you rather die in the wilderness? Do you want to be part of the majority that would rather die than change? Or, are you willing to give up your past ways for God's ways of thinking?

If you are willing to change the spirit of your mind, you can stop being a slave to your old thoughts and begin to prosper. If you are willing, you can leave Egypt behind and start living in your promised land. However, the *spirit of your mind* must change.

The *spirit of your mind* also affects your physical body as well as your behavior, attitudes, and actions toward others. In Proverbs 17:22, the Word says that a merry heart does as much good for you as medicine does, but a broken spirit will cause your bones to dry up. If your heart — the spirit of your mind — is positive and happy, then your physical body will be stronger and healthier. If your heart is negative, pessimistic, always seeing the bad, your physical body will dry up.

I knew someone who went through this kind of thing. In fact, she believed that God brought bad things into her life, and that He was part of her problem. She believed He caused her to be sick in order for her to develop spiritually and become more compassionate. That negative *spirit of her mind* caused her body to manifest physical symptoms. Her bones dried up. She developed rheumatoid arthritis, and her joints began to become stiff. Her bones became fragile. I do not understand all of the details of her condition, but very soon, she was stiff, pain-ridden, and greatly depressed. Because I knew her well, it was easy for me to trace the cause of her physical problem to the condition of the *spirit of her mind.*

Another illustration that I saw was a young boy who lived near my family when I was a child. My brother and I grew up with horses and cattle. We were rambunctious "little critters" ourselves. When we left the house in the morning, we might end up anywhere on the ranch. We could end up riding horses or steers, walking fences, or making tree forts.

Our parents never worried about us too much. But our neighbor boy's family was very concerned over him. They constantly watched him, guarded him, and protected him. They worried over the least little thing. They were afraid to have him play in the field — he might fall down. They were afraid for him to climb a tree — he might fall out of it. He was smothered.

Before he was out of his teen years, he died. They were not exactly sure what killed him, it was not a disease or a condition. I believe what really happened was that he was smothered to death. He was killed by his parents' fearful, negative *state of mind.*

So again I ask you: Do you really want a new life? Or do you want to just continue on with what you have had for years and years?

Six Steps To Renewing the Mind

In the next chapter, I want to discuss these six steps. They are:

1) You must have a strong desire to change.

You will not change because someone else wants you to or is telling you to change.

2) You must increase your knowledge of life, yourself, and your potential.

3) You must diligently apply these truths day after day after day.

4) You must defend your new state of mind against your old ways of thinking and against limitations people want to place on you.

They may say, "It won't work. You can't do it." Or you may say to yourself, "I'll never make it." You will have to learn to defend yourself against your old limitations.

5) You need to dissociate yourself from some of the people from your past.

You will have to separate yourself from anyone who tries to keep you from achieving the desire of your heart.

6) You must depend on God.

Even though this is listed as the last step, it is the first. You have to depend on God to change the spirit of your mind. Renewing the mind takes more than knowledge, more than psychology, more than desire and human effort. It takes the work of the Lord. Jesus is the One Who gives us the ability to change.

4

The Process of Change

Many people want change, if it can happen "right now." But change is not defined or confined by time. *Change is a process* that must continue if the desired result is to be reached. *Change* is a lifestyle that we adopt and begin to function in for the rest of our existence.

Renewing the spirit of the mind is not easy, yet it is something everyone can do, and it will produce lasting change. But I am not giving you some get-rich-quick scheme, or some easy program to follow.

As an example, look at diet programs. If you fast or take certain drugs, you might lose a lot of weight in a few weeks. But you know how that turns out. The same eating habits that put the weight on in the first place will cause you to gain it back very soon. But when you change your thinking about food, you can change your eating habits, and the results will be lasting.

Your subconscious, your reflex-thought system, could be called the root of the mind. It is the system under the surface that is not seen, but that controls what happens in your life.

Proverbs 23:7 says **as he** (a man or woman) **thinketh in his heart, so is he** This could be paraphrased this way: As the spirit of your mind is, so your conscious mind is, so all of your life is. If your heart is filled with negativity, then your life will be filled with it also. We must let Jesus help us change our hearts so our lives can change.

The spirit of your mind is like the foundation of a great skyscraper. The depth of the foundation dictates its height. What is underground controls what can be constructed above ground. That is exactly what the spirit of your mind does: It controls what is manifested in your life. The spirit of your mind controls your attitudes and ultimately all of your actions.

The spirit of your mind is not rational or reasonable, because it does not contain the reasoning faculty of your mind. That is in the conscious mind. Ideally, we would reason things out, find the truth and the good about everything in our conscious minds, *then* file the truth away as a program to trigger or control our behavior.

However, in the environment in which we live, this is not possible. The best we can do is change the negative information we have filed away so that we operate on the correct program.

I want to show you how to recognize when you are operating from negatively stored information, and help you to change the abundance of your heart to thinking based on the principles of God. (Matt. 12:35.)

You need to understand that what is in your subconscious is not necessarily true. It does not have to be true for the spirit of your mind to believe it and act on it. Many people do things that are totally irrational and unreasonable, but that is the way they learned to think, so they continue to act on those negative programs.

Look at how many Americans have credit problems and how the majority of people handle finances. Is it reasonable? No. But it is the prevailing spirit of the mind in this country, so most people continue to handle money unwisely. Before World War II, the spirit of the mind in finances was to *not* owe anything. The credit syndrome really began after the 1940s, and it continues to flourish even though it is an unreasonable way to handle money.

Look at abusive parents. Most of them know child abuse is irrational, irresponsible, and wrong. Yet they continue to do it, because most of them were abused themselves, and the program that *children are to be abused* is written heavily in their subconscious minds. That false, negative program controls their actions, although they do not want to be abusive.

A Strong Desire To Change

As I listed in Chapter 3, the first step in making a change in the spirit of your mind is *to desire* a change, not just admit you need a change. You can admit that you need to change but still never change. Knowing you need to change is not a basis for solid and lasting change. It takes a strong desire, a *determination* to change.

Knowing you need to change may affect some of the external functional things, but your basic internal thoughts will not change. Changing the external without changing the internal will only be a "cosmetic change." It is like putting makeup over blemishes.

For example, you know you need to drive within the speed limit, and you make an effort to do so. But if you slip, then you remind yourself by saying, "I am going to stay within the speed limit, because I know I need to." So you have to *make* yourself do that day after day. You have to consciously think about not letting your foot get a little heavy, and you have to keep an eye on the speedometer. But, if you changed the spirit of your mind from running at your own speed to running at the legal speed by *desiring* to stay within the limit, you would exchange one control program for another. You would automatically always stay within the speed limit, without having to consciously think about it all of the time.

Many times, in our family or marriage relationships, we do what we ought to do, but our actions and attitudes never become a desire. Therefore, we constantly are having to force ourselves to do what is right, but we never enjoy it. This is why many divorces occur. We do things because we ought to, but not because we want to. Then, doing what we ought to do finally gets to be more trouble than it is worth. But if we know how to change the spirit of our minds from "a duty performed against our will," to a desire to make the marriage work and make our spouse happy, divorce would never occur.

Desire is the motivation of life. What you desire, you will be strongly motivated to pursue. Only what you desire will you pursue over the long term. So build a desire for the things you want into your mind — not just a "should," or a "need."

The next thing I am sure you want to know is: "How do I build a desire?" You begin by "wanting to want to" do something.

You might say, "I don't really *want* to lose weight, but I know that I should." If you operate with that thinking, you will not lose weight, or if you do, you will gain it back. You might say, "I do not want to change my spending habits, but I know that I should." This thinking will not bring permanent changes into your finances.

The way to change the spirit of your mind is to change the "ought to" to "want to" by beginning to say to yourself, "I *want to have a desire* to change my eating habits (or my spending habits)." Then before long, you will have the desire, and you can begin to say, "I *want to change* my attitude about food (or money)." And finally, you will find not only that you really do want to change, but that you *have* changed. Then you will begin to see lasting results. You will no longer have to think about eating or spending money. Your eating and spending will be controlled by a positive program in the spirit of your mind.

So the first step in renewing the spirit of your mind is to create a desire to change.

Deepen Your Knowledge

The second step is *to deepen your knowledge* of yourself and your world. Your knowledge base must increase for your life experience to increase. Your knowledge base is the foundation on which you are building, and if your knowledge base is shallow or small, your life experience will be shallow or small.

Scientists say we use, at the maximum, about ten percent of our brain capacity. Most of us use about five percent; some of us use less. If we expand the use of our conscious minds, that would expand the subconscious, and our awareness of the potential within us will be greater. We would have an expanded awareness of opportunity, an awareness of what life can be. Then we would begin to seek after those things, desire those things, and experience those things. If your mind is so limited that you do not even realize what is available, and what your potential is, then you will never strive for those things.

Here are six ways to *deepen your knowledge base:*

1. Correspondence courses.

2. Books, tapes, and videos.

3. Local programs, such as community colleges and seminars.

4. Church classes.

5. Private research in libraries.

6. Job-training opportunities.

There are literally thousands of correspondence programs that can be studied in your home, and there are many more thousands of books, tapes, and videos available. If you simply spend a couple of hours a day reading, listening to tapes, or watching videos, you can gain accurate, positive, and effective knowledge. This can be done a few minutes at a time throughout the day as you are preparing for work, driving to the grocery store, and so forth.

Attending local educational programs, seminars, and conferences does take more time, but if you will spend that time, it will be well worth it. You will gain knowledge of people, information about current events, and knowledge of spiritual things.

Most people live within a short distance of some public library. Become a member and learn how to use the facilities that are free to everyone A librarian will be glad to show you how to use the card indexes and even how to do basic research. Get a notebook for each subject. You might start with something that is of great interest to you. Spending an hour or so once a week, or every two weeks, is something most of us can find time to do *if we really have a desire to deepen our knowledge base.*

Finally, if your company is offering training sessions, take advantage of them, even if they are not in your specific area of work. You will very seldom find that any knowledge you have gained is wasted. Any way that you can deepen your knowledge base will enable you to grow and change. You will be affecting the spirit of your mind.

Remember: the spirit of your mind was well established during the first fourteen or fifteen years of your life. That is when most people stop learning. They may expand existing knowledge, but comparatively few people deepen their knowledge after that age. Most college work, for example, simply expands the things already known. A small percentage of college work presents completely new knowledge.

If you force yourself to deepen your knowledge base, you will soon have a desire to learn, and that will affect the spirit of your mind.

Diligently Apply the Truths You Learn

You change or renew the spirit of your mind through *diligence.*

- Diligently think new thoughts.

- Diligently seek new ways.

- Diligently apply yourself to grow and to change.

Most people fail in the process of renewal because they will not be consistent in this third step. They will not constantly affirm the changes. They will not persevere. You may think saying, or affirming, something is vain — and it is — if the words are empty with no belief behind them. But, by diligently speaking out loud your desire to want to change, then your desire to change, you build faith.

Faith comes by hearing, the Word says. (Rom. 10:17.) We sometimes hear this verse quoted, "Faith comes by hearing and hearing and hearing." Hearing yourself say these changes is part of the process of building your faith. Then changes *can* occur, and it becomes possible for you to change your attitudes and behavior.

As I said in the beginning of this chapter, renewing the spirit of your mind is not an overnight plan. It is a lifetime plan. Renewing your mind is a lifestyle in itself, and to achieve your purpose, you must be diligent.

There is a saying that illustrates this concept: The only way you can eat an elephant is one bite at a time. So the only way you can renew your mind is "one bite," one change, at a time. You must stay at the process day after day after day. It took a number of years to build your subconscious. It may take years to renew it, taking one change at a time. People spend half their lifetimes developing negative habits, then they want to change them overnight. It does not work that way. You built the spirit of your mind as a daily process, and you must renew it as a daily process.

If you will be diligent, I guarantee that you will see changes occur. But if you want to see results immediately, then the renewing process will not work for you.

Defend Against the Old Thoughts

The fourth step is *to defend your mind* against the old thoughts, the old attitudes, and the old behaviors.

Just because you desire to change old thinking to new ways of thinking does not mean the old ways will automatically "fall off." Those old habits and ways of thinking will resurface time after time, sometimes for years. The tendencies will be there to slip into the old bad attitude, the old sharp tongue, the old desire to just give up and throw in the towel. Those old thoughts are like deep roots that keep popping up. Even if you pour a slab of concrete over them, they will creep through a crack in the concrete and resurface.

You have to defend yourself. Defend your mind. Defend your thoughts against those old attitudes that come back to you. You also need to understand, that even though they keep coming back, it does not mean that you have not changed; it *does not mean* you are not making progress. When that old way of thinking resurfaces, do not say, "I've been working on this for so long, I've been trying to change this for so long, it does not seem I am making any progress." Just keep on going, and put that old thought aside one more time. Every time you defend against that old way of thinking, you strengthen the new way. Every time you allow the old way to come back, you weaken the new way.

If you do not defend yourself, the old thoughts *will* come back, and you will find yourself going through the routine so many Christians do. That is, change for two weeks, then go back to the old. We tend to get excited over the new — new program, new diet, new tape, new message — and for a couple of weeks, we are all "fired up." We are "going for it." Then suddenly we find ourselves back to the same old habits and routines. Instead of being diligent about changing, we go looking for another new diet, tape, or program.

How do you defend yourself against the old thoughts? You develop reminders for yourself. When you have had a way of thinking for a period of years, you can be overtaken by it before you realize it. You may have had a bad habit of using a sharp tongue toward your family or fellow employees. You must realize there is a way of thinking that goes along with a sharp tongue and a bad attitude. That way of thinking begins long before the words are spoken. You can stop yourself from saying anything. As one of the Proverbs says, "If you have thought evil, put your hand over your mouth." (Prov. 30:32.) Now you have set a reminder on guard in your conscious mind: "As soon as I recognize a negative thought, I will not speak it. I will 'cast down' (2 Cor. 10:5) that invalid thought."

Dissociate From the Past

This fifth step is an area that most people do not like to hear about. Many of us want to hang on to longtime relationships in spite of the fact that they are not beneficial; in fact, they may have been detrimental. There are people in your life from whom you must dissociate yourself, if you want to change.

If you continue in the same old relationships, you will continue with the same old lifestyle. But, if you want a new lifestyle, you must take the fifth step: create a new circle of friends.

Some years ago, I decided I was going to have a completely new life. I had been an "average" young American. I enjoyed smoking pot, drinking beer, going to parties. I went to work and got my paycheck, but I also wanted to have a good time. I enjoyed being "loaded" and having different girlfriends. I liked driving a car with fancy "mags" and being "cool."

I was into the "hip" scene, snorting cocaine like everyone else I knew — just having a good old time like so many people do today. It was not a drug problem, or a drinking or smoking problem; it was a lifestyle.

As you probably know, you do not stop snorting cocaine or drinking or even smoking cigarettes by dealing with the tobacco or alcohol. You have to deal with your lifestyle. The attitudes that allow you to enjoy that kind of life must be changed.

So when I said, "I am going to change," I got involved with people who could teach, train, and help me develop a new lifestyle. Soon I realized that the development of this new lifestyle meant I was going to have to develop a whole new circle of friends, because the people I had been with for so many years were not thinking about changing. They were not interested in doing anything different with their lives.

Every time I was with them, I was pulled back into the old habits, back into the old ways. If I talked to them about changing, they took it as "a put-down," a criticism. So I was not welcomed if I wanted to talk about change and becoming a different person.

Eventually, I had to dissociate myself from them and it was difficult. I really did not want to, because they were my friends, my old buddies. We had been together since high school. We had done so much together. I cared about them, and they cared about me.

Yet, I realized that if I wanted a renewed spirit of mind and a new lifestyle, I would have to leave my old friends. You, too, will have to accept the fact that your desire to change will separate you from some old friends. You will have to develop a new circle of friends.

Most people in your life will not like your changing your lifestyle. In fact, there were many people I knew who would rather have had me using drugs, drinking beer, and throwing away my money, than to have me create a new life and begin to prosper and enjoy myself.

Why did they feel that way? Because they resented what was happening to me, and because they did not want to change. They wanted to stay the way they were, and the contrast with my new lifestyle made them uncomfortable.

If you keep hanging around people who do not want to change and grow, they will steal the desire and motivation from you. You will eventually give up and stay in the same old rut. Do you know what a rut is? It is a grave with both ends kicked out and there is room to get a lot of people in there with you.

The old adage is true: "Misery loves company." Many people would rather have you stay poor, negative, and unhappy than to have you change and begin to enjoy life. So dissociate from old friends who will not change, and begin to build a new circle of friends, a group of people who are going where you are going, doing what you are doing, seeking what you are seeking. In that crowd, you will find support, help, strength, and motivation.

Depend on God and Others for Support

Renewing the spirit of your mind is not something you can do by yourself. This process must be done with the help of the Holy Spirit, or it will not work. You must also have the support and help of people around you. So when you replace that old circle of friends, choose new ones who are in agreement with what you are doing, and who are willing to help you. You are not a hermit or an "island unto yourself." You need God, and you need friends. You cannot change yourself by yourself. You *can* change with the help of God. You cannot counsel yourself. Negative thinking cannot straighten out negative thinking.

Build a support base. Believe that God wants your life to be blessed. God is not part of your problem. He is your answer. God is not against you. He is not trying to keep the good things of life from you. He wants you to be blessed. Depend on Him to provide for you and to make a way for you.

Each one of us, whether we want to admit it or not, is part of a body. (1 Cor. 12:12-26.) And, just as in the physical body, one part can do little without the other parts. As a part, you can be strong and effective. If you separate yourself from other parts of the body, you will accomplish little, enjoy little, and not have the life you desire.

Perhaps you have said, "I am going to be my own person. I don't need anybody. I'm going where I want to go. I'm going to do what I want to do. I will be free and independent." What that means is that you are going to be in bondage to loneliness and isolation. This sixth step is a very important one: depend on God and on others in the Body of Christ.

A Prerequisite for Renewing the Mind

Before the spirit of your mind can change, the real you must change. You are more than a soul (mind, will, and emotions) and a body. You are a spirit being who lives in a body and has a soul that you want renewed in the spirit of your mind. First, however, the spirit being — the real you — must be changed into a new creation.

If you have already accepted Jesus as your Savior, you have been made a new creation, a spirit being infused with the life of God and in whom Jesus lives through the Holy Spirit. The real you, the spirit being, is made in the image of God, and you must have the life of God in you to be made new. This change is immediate. It is instantaneous, and a very simple process! This change God does for you. You simply have to accept His gift of a new you. God has given *new life* through Jesus. Your only part is to receive it.

You receive His life by confessing out loud:

"Jesus, I believe You are the Son of God, the Creator of the universe and mankind. (Rom. 10:9,10.) I accept the sacrifice of your life on Calvary as payment for my own transgressions. (John 3:16.) I ask you to forgive my sins, and I now accept that forgiveness. I ask you to make me a new creation. (2 Cor. 5:17.) I make You the Lord of my life. I will depend on you to provide new life, new strength, forgiveness, and help for me."

This simple faith and trust in Jesus will open the door for the Holy Spirit to give you a recreated spirit. That will be the beginning for an entirely new realm of life. It works. I am living it, and I see it in thousands of people around me every week. It will happen for you.

Now that you are a new person, your spirit is new. You are ready to move forward and use the information in this book to renew your mind, which will then shape your circumstances and your future.

The next four chapters will move from instruction to training. I want to help you go beyond the academic knowledge of changing the spirit of your mind and into the experience of doing it. You will need to have paper and pencil for the next chapters.

5

Believe That You *Can* Change

In this chapter, you will need paper and something to write with. Also, I suggest you read this in a quiet place where you can meditate on what you read.

You have already seen how your thinking controls the way you act, which ultimately controls the way you live. The way you believe or think controls the way you are. Therefore, the way you see *yourself* determines what you will do with your life.

Remember, it does not matter to your subconscious control center if what you think is true or false. If you have believed something about yourself, that is filed away in your subconscious as truth, whether it is or not. If you think it, it becomes "true" in your life, whether or not it is reasonable or rational.

So by renewing the spirit of your mind, you renew your whole life. By changing the way you think about yourself, you change the way you deal with your life.

Strengths and Weaknesses

I would like you to start off by considering your strengths and your weaknesses.

How do you esteem yourself at this time?

What is the value you have placed on yourself?

It is very important to begin renewing the mind with an understanding of the way you see yourself.

Strengths are the talents, qualities, characteristics, and abilities that "come naturally" to you; the things you do without really trying. We all have areas where we are strong.

Perhaps you are a strong communicator or a strong listener; perhaps you are good at doing things with your hands; perhaps you are good at planning, organizing, and administrating.

At the same time, everyone has areas of weakness, things that do not just flow naturally for us. We might like to do those things, but we cannot — or we cannot without great effort. Perhaps you always wanted to be musical, but you just are not.

Now take a moment, and write down five of your strengths, five areas where you are strong, or five talents. Then write down five weaknesses. Take time to really think about these ten things and be honest. Do not just skip over this, because listing these things will establish how you value yourself at this time. Then we can move on and do some changing from where you are right now.

I want to talk to you about what you have just done as if I were a counselor sitting with you face to face. I want to ask you a few questions:

Was this difficult for you to do, or relatively easy?

If it was difficult, it could be that you do not really know yourself. Perhaps you have never taken the time to look for the things you do well. If weaknesses were easiest for you to list, then your thinking has been programmed predominantly with the things you do wrong, or the things you do not do well. You have focused on those, instead of your strengths.

This is something you need to make a decision on right now. You need to *choose* to focus on your strengths, the things that are going to move you forward in life. Your weaknesses are not going to cause you to prosper. Your weaknesses will not cause you to build a good marriage or a good family.

Focus on the strengths. Say this out loud: "I will focus on my strengths." Say it again: "I will focus on my strengths!"

Focus on the Strengths

In the last chapter, we talked about rejecting your old thoughts. In order to see those weaknesses turned around and made into strengths, it is necessary to *reject* them from your life.

For example, if you are a quiet person, you may think that is a weakness because you do not communicate, you do not come out of yourself and share with others. However, as you examine your life and make these decisions, that weakness can be changed.

Begin to think about yourself as a good listener, not a bad communicator. Instead of thinking of yourself as quiet and shy, begin to think of yourself as one who is able to listen. People who really know how to listen are rare. A good listener can learn more than one who talks all the time. A good listener can know people and empathize with them.

Or suppose you have thought that you are not smart. You do not believe you have the mental capabilities other people have. I want you to begin to see that changing. If you are a hard worker, then you need to see that you can accomplish your goals in life through hard work — and many times, hard work will accomplish more and get you farther than having a high intelligence. So do not concentrate on the weakness. Turn it into a strength, and begin to say to yourself: "I am not a slow learner. I am not dumb. I am a hard worker."

Using the principles I have shown you on how to turn weaknesses into strengths, write down five positive responses, or five positive ways, those five weaknesses could be viewed. You do not have to figure out all the details or be specific. Above all, do not let negative thinking tell you, "This is not going to work. It is not going to make a bit of difference. I have always been dumb, and I will always be dumb."

You must stop that line of thought right now.

Finding ways to turn those weaknesses into strengths will begin to renew the spirit of your mind about yourself. It will help you to begin to reject those weaknesses.

Another thing to remember is if you focus on your own weaknesses, you probably focus on the weaknesses of others as well. Focusing on the negative causes you to judge others and to focus on the negative things about them as well. This is the beginning of relationship failure. In order for your relationships to prosper and be strong, you need to focus on your strengths and those of the other people involved.

Now look at the five strengths you wrote down. Even if you thought you had no special talents, when you look for your good points, you will see things about yourself that you have overlooked. You do have special qualities and talents that others do not have. You are unique and special in many ways.

Look at each of those five strengths and imagine what you can do with each of them. For example, if you wrote down that you are a quick thinker, imagine what would happen if you developed that trait. You might be a valuable person in a public relations department, or handling complaints. You would also be very valuable in a busy office or a phone center where there are many calls and decisions must be made on the spot. With training and experience, you could become a very valuable person in that situation. Or you might work in a day-care center where there are many children, where decisions must be made quickly about their care. The strength of quick thinking would be of great value.

Begin to think of areas where you would really "shine," if you could just take those strengths and use them. Do not think small. Do not limit yourself. Look at the first thing you wrote down, stop reading, and just think about it for a few minutes. Picture yourself using that strength in various settings. Then go on to the next one.

Now that you have seen yourself using those strengths, and doing the things that could be done with the qualities you have, begin to expand or enhance those strengths and weaknesses-turned-strengths.

List all of the adjectives (descriptive words) that you can think of to describe the person you have just been thinking about. Sharp? Beautiful? Handsome? Quick on their feet? Fast and efficient? Effective? Prosperous?

What are the ways you would describe that person if it were not you but someone else? How would you describe yourself if you were doing everything that could be done with the qualities and characteristics that are unique to you? What would you call that person? How would you describe that person?

A Thirty-Day Exercise

Here is an assignment you can do for the next thirty days. Each day, take out that list of strengths, and weaknesses made into strengths, and read them out loud to yourself. If you will do that every day for the next month, you will begin to focus on your strengths. Then you will begin to see yourself living within those strengths, using them and producing results in your life.

What will happen is the value you place on yourself will increase. You will see yourself doing the things you have always wanted to do and becoming the person you really can be. Instead of focusing on the weaknesses, you will be focusing on the strengths that will enhance them. It will only take you a few minutes each day, but you will be reprogramming your mind. You will be renewing the spirit of your mind.

It is important to say positive things about yourself. Do not say the things that tear down and destroy your self-worth. Every time you say something negative, you are strengthening your weaknesses. You are hurting yourself. Every time you say something positive, you are strengthening your strengths. You are building and helping yourself.

Begin to say: "I can accomplish what I desire to do. I am sharp. My mind is clear. When I do a job, I do it right, I do it fast, and I do it well."

If you continue to say those things out loud, you will begin to believe them, and they will begin to come true in your life. Hearing yourself say them will help you even more than hearing someone else say them.

When you do this, you will be taking responsibility for the way you are. Let me remind you of the six steps to the renewing of the spirit of the mind:

1. Desire to change.

2. Deepen your knowledge base.

3. Be diligent. Follow through with the exercises listed in this chapter. Do not give up.

4. Defend your mind against your old thoughts, old habits, and old ways of thinking. Fight them off, and do not let yourself fall into the old routines.

5. Dissociate. Get away from people who would keep you in the old pattern, people who tell you that you cannot change or who try to keep you from changing.

6. Depend on God and on positive people around you to support you.

As you progress, you will find your list of strengths growing and your list of weaknesses shrinking. When your own self-evaluation improves, a new confidence will lift you into situations, relationships, and opportunities you could not have imagined available to you before.

6
Mental and Physical Fitness

You will also need paper and pencil in this chapter. It would be helpful to be somewhere quiet without distractions in order to really benefit from the information I am sharing.

Mental fitness, as well as physical fitness, is a major key to obtaining peace and prosperity in your life. To be fit is to be sound, healthy, and able to cope with the pressures of life without ill effects. Many people have not learned to deal with daily pressures, so they are experiencing negative effects in their minds and bodies regularly. Doctors see millions of people who are experiencing sicknesses, diseases, and psychological disorders because of the mental and physical pressures of everyday life.

Mental stress is reflected in anxiety, worry, arguing or fighting with those around us, and it usually is expressed to the ones closest to us, the ones we care about the most. Mental pressure also shows up as difficulty in sleeping, and in anger and frustration when facing simple everyday things such as traffic jams, or long lines at the bank or checkout counters. Confusion and doubts about the future, or about one's ability to handle the children or other responsibilities, are other symptoms of mental pressure. Still other symptoms might be the desire to get away, to leave everything behind, or not wanting to deal with things any longer.

Many times, divorces are the result of people reaching a breaking point in dealing with stress. They think their marriage is the problem instead of realizing the problems are symptoms of mental and physical stress from other areas of life. Sometimes, the separation will not be marriage but a "divorce" from a job or a place. People think getting a new spouse, a new job, or moving to a new city will solve their problems. However, escape only means exchanging one set of pressure for another.

Physical symptoms many times are reflections of stress and pressure: headaches, back and neck aches, stomach problems, ulcers, chest pains, fatigue, shortness of breath, overweight or underweight. Those things should not be part of our lives; yet they often are. We need to deal with our mental and physical problems. We can have victory by going through some exercises to bring fitness to mind and body. Then we will enter a new phase of life that is much more exciting and fulfilling.

Rearrange Your Priorities

The first step to fitness is to take a look at your schedule. What have you committed yourself to do? What is taking up your time? More than likely, you need to do some rearranging of your priorities.

You determine your top priority by figuring out what you spend the most time doing. Very often, people are not aware they have established priorities, so their time is absorbed with things they do not really want, or need to be doing. If this is the case in your life, it will not take long before your priorities are out of kilter and your life is out of balance.

The first thing to do is to write down the present arrangement of your priorities. Do this by examining your schedule. Find out what you spend the most time doing, and put that at the top of the list. Then see what you spend the next largest amount of time doing, and list that second — and so forth.

In looking at your list you may find that your job is number one — making money, getting a promotion, doing what the company demands that you do. Continue down the list, and see what place your family has, what place God has, and where the exercise of mind and body fits in. If you will be honest with yourself and take time to do this, you will be on the way to developing mental and physical fitness.

Assuming that you — like myself and most other people — do have some priorities out of place, I have provided some questions that will help you recognize what areas are out of balance.

Who is in control of your time? Write down what you believe.

Who decides what is a priority for you?

What would you have to change in order to reorganize your time and priorities?

What is hindering you from reorganizing your time and priorities?

Very often, we allow the boss, the job, or the company for which we work to become the controlling factor in our lives. Perhaps I should say that money is the bottom line for many of us. The need for finances controls our time, and our relationship with our spouse and children. We are more dedicated to making money than to anything else. Of course, we need money to live. However, many times, men will say they are work-aholics for the good of their families when, in reality, the wives and children would rather have fewer things and more time and attention.

A lot of men realize their mistakes when it is too late: when the divorces are final, the heart attacks happen, or failures of some other sort occur. Then they realize that their priorities have been out of alignment so long that some kind of destruction has occurred.

So be honest with yourself in answering those four questions, especially number four: What is stopping you from reorganizing the priorities in your life? If it is your job, you may have to quit that job, because your life is more important than making money. If it is some other person, or relationship, you need to examine the situation and bring about the change that is necessary.

Now I want to give you six priorities upon which your schedule should be built. You can use these in a variety of ways, and of course, you should apply them to what works for you personally. It is a very positive list that has been used by many successful people in every type of lifestyle.

Six Important Priorities

The number one priority is Jesus and *faith* in Him. You must have a right relationship with God, and you must have your life built on a spiritual foundation. There are too many pressures, too many difficult circumstances to try to handle on your own. Your first priority must be your faith life.

The second one is *mental and physical fitness.* You need time for the exercising of your mind and body. If you do not have time to care for your mind and body, you will not have time for your job or your family. You may die young.

Number three is *family.* Before finances, before jobs, and other commitments of life, you must make time for your family. If you do not have a successful relationship with your husband or your wife, then your life is very shallow. If you cannot enjoy your children, spend time with them as they grow up, enjoy those early school years, the camping, walks, and hikes — if you cannot do that, then your life is out of order, and you will live a very shallow existence.

Number four is *fellowship.* This includes your relationships with other people and with people in your church. Having friendships and involvements with people are more important than the savings account, the position at the company, or our status in society. What good is a high status without friends? What good is having a large bank account but no one to enjoy it with? Fellowship with other people is extremely important.

The fifth thing on the list of those who are successful is *finance.* It is important to make money, to meet the needs of your family, but it should not be the number one priority. Making money must be viewed from the proper perspective of your life. Money can be a positive influence, a tool with which to accomplish things, if it is kept in the proper perspective with everything else. If money becomes your first love, it becomes the "root of all evil." (1 Tim. 6:10.) The Bible does not say *money* is the root of all evil, but that *the love of money* is the destructive force.

Number six is simply *having fun*. The old saying that "all work and no play makes Jack a dull boy" is very true. Without fun and relaxation, your faculties become dulled. You do not "take time to smell the roses" or to enjoy the world around you. You should enjoy the life God has given you and the friends He has placed around you. Find a hobby, something you enjoy. Perhaps this can be combined with family activities.

Compare these six priorities with your present priorities, then see what changes you can make to get your priorities into the proper order. You may not be able to do this all at once but you can begin to work on them one at a time to get your present priorities replaced.

The Beginning of Mental Fitness

Once your priorities are in order, mental fitness begins with removing worry, anxiety, and doubt. As we have discussed in the first few chapters of this book, what happens in your mind controls what happens in your life.

In order to be able to live according to your new priorities, you must get negative thinking out of your life. Worry is one of the most negative forms of thinking there is. Worry is actually having faith that something bad is going to happen. *Worry is negative faith.*

Mental fitness begins with getting the worry and other negative beliefs out of your mind. You may think you are "naturally" a pessimist. But you were not born worrying. You were not born a pessimist. You were born without a care. You were born with the capacity to believe good things were going to happen every day. You *learned* how to worry. With help from parents or others around you, you trained yourself to worry.

Get your pencil and paper out again, and write down ten things you worry about. Do not take time to study or figure them out, but quickly and honestly write them down. Perhaps you worry about getting your bills paid, about the condition of your company, about your physical health, about your weight, your children, your house and needed repairs, and other things like these.

Now take a good look at those ten things. Put a check mark by those over which you have some kind of control. Draw a line through each one over which you have no control.

Take a few minutes and look carefully at those which you could do something about. Consider what you could do if you looked at those things objectively, as solvable problems, and not as chronic worries. If your house is a mess, could you change your own habits and use of time? Could you get your family involved in helping? Could you cut expenses elsewhere and hire someone to clean? What could you do to keep your house clean every day, and how would you feel if it were that way?

If you are worrying about your weight, what could you do to gain or lose? Could you exercise more? Could you change your eating habits, and the kinds of things you eat?

As you take each of the things you checked and analyze them in this way, you will turn negative things into positive ones, just as you turn weaknesses into strengths.

Next, take the things that are crossed out, and erase them from your mind. If you need to, go back and reread the first four chapters of this book to see how to remove thoughts from your mind. Use that information right now with the first "worry" you crossed out.

Perhaps your worry is the neighbors, or the state of the stock market, or bank interest rates, or maybe even the weather. Whatever it is, I want you to say: "I take no thought about _____" (insert your "worry"). Say it out loud again, and once again.

Now take a look at the rest of your list of worries that you can do nothing about and begin to replace those negative thoughts with positive ones. Say, "I take no thought about the neighbor's dog, or the condition of their yard, or the stock market, or bank interest rates," and continue through each one on your list.

Go through that list twice, saying "I take no thought" about each of them. It is important to do this, so stop reading and take the time to do it now.

Proper Mental Food

Mental fitness continues with proper feeding of the mind. If you are not feeding your mind, it will get weak just as your body will, if it is not fed. If you go for a day or two without feeding your body, you will begin to get tired and weak. If you fast long enough, your body will cease to function; you will die.

Many of our minds have been on a fast, and perhaps if the mind has not been fed nor trained, it is getting weak and tired. Someone said, "My mind has been on 'birth-control pills' for a long time!" That well describes the average person, who has not given birth to a new thought in years. One of your first priorities in renewing the spirit of your mind is to begin to get your mind in shape. Get it strong, active, and healthy. Mental fitness comes with proper feeding and exercising of the mind.

The first step in feeding your mind is to remove what I call "space-out" time. That is the time you waste mentally by watching worthless television programs. This does not sharpen your mental capacity; it is a waste of mental energy and is "space-out" time. You are acting no differently than the child whose mind is captivated by a video game or children's program, oblivious to what is going on around him. He is just absorbing junk food into his mind.

For you, it might be television or radio, novels or magazines. Some people try to live off mental junk food. In order to renew the spirit of your mind, you must break the junk-food habit and get rid of "space-out" time. You must begin to control what is going into your mind and what you are doing with your mind.

Scheduling the feeding of your mind is as important as scheduling your lunch, your job activities, your physical exercise. You must plan to feed your mind, otherwise your mind is going to atrophy. Your mind will be wasted. Your mind will become so lazy that you will not be able to create, or come up with the ideas, opportunities, thoughts, plans, and knowledge necessary to succeed and prosper in life.

Four Ways of Feeding the Mind

The number one way to feed the mind is to *read*. You need to make time in your schedule to read, and you must pick material that will bring positive motivation into your life. There are so many published materials that are not "junk food," so many *good* books that will inspire you and cause you to grow. Do not waste time reading garbage. Read material that will help you in your field of endeavor.

Number two is *schedule time to listen*. Listen to cassette tapes, that contain positive teaching material that will move you, stir you, feed you, and challenge you. We could include videos in this, because there are many good videos you could watch instead of watching worthless television shows.

Number three is *study*. Look for study materials that will help you in your field of work, or will help you with your family. If you are a parent, get some good books on parenting. Anyone who wants to raise a dog to be obedient and fun to be around, will go out and buy a book on dog care. However, many of us never bother to look for information on rearing our children, something with much greater significance.

Read the book, then sit down with your spouse at least once a week and discuss what you have read. Study these materials. You might get a book on something your child is interested in, and then say to that child, "Let's talk about this a little bit and see how we can get you where you want to be with it."

Number four is *imagination*. You have an imagination, whether you use it or not. Like I said earlier, some of us have not given birth to anything in so long that our imaginations are inactive. However, you can stir up your imagination and begin to create new ideas and opportunities.

How can you improve the quality of your life? How can you improve your relationships? How can your job be different or better? Everything that has been initiated in the world began as a creation in someone's imagination. You have a mind too — just like the inventors and innovators you have admired in the past. Your mind can create in your own world, your own sphere of influence. You just have to take time to imagine.

Write into your weekly schedule one way you can improve in each of these four areas.

Physical Fitness Also Is Important

To be physically fit is as important as being mentally fit. In fact, your physical fitness controls the quality of your lifestyle. Overweight, tired, and weak people cannot do what they want to do. They cannot live the standard of life they really want to live.

All of us tend to develop excuses, rationalizations, and justifications about not exercising. We tend to excuse ourselves until we get to the point where we are living far below the standard we want to have. If you will be honest with yourself, you will realize that when you are physically unfit, you cannot live the life you really want to live. You cannot do what you really would like to do. I am not talking about only those who are overweight. Being underweight can hinder you just as much as being the right weight, but being flabby and having poor muscle tone.

Here are some general questions you can answer regarding physical fitness:

Why have you allowed physical weaknesses to develop?

Why have you avoided exercise?

Why have you allowed yourself to become easily fatigued and short of breath after physical activity?

I believe you will find the answer falls into one of five categories:

- Are you lazy?

- Are you unaware of the situation?

- Are you harboring a "death wish" to the extent that you have just given up on life?

- Are you avoiding other people or circumstances?

- Are anger and frustration controlling you to the point that eating and retreating into sleeping or becoming a "couch potato" are your tranquilizers?

In order to help yourself, you must be totally honest. You need to answer these questions objectively. If you will be honest about what has caused you to allow physical weakness to take over your life, you will be on the way to changing the situation and to turning your life around.

Perhaps you have tried to change before and have not been able to do so. In that case, what you need to find out is what caused you to fail. Like a lot of other people, you have tried diets, started exercise programs, bought memberships to health clubs, or gone through different programs to get your body in shape.

I want to give you another list of possibilities to examine that will enable you — if you answer honestly — to see clearly the cause of your failures:

- You never *really* tried to change, just made a "token" attempt.

- You did not persevere and only stayed at it for a week or two. Your attempts to change have never been consistent or long-term.

- Your environment, the people around you, made it too difficult. Peer pressure to not change kept you from changing.

- You never really felt a need to change, never saw the benefits of becoming physically fit.

Again, be honest with yourself. Consider each of these possibilities and see if one of them is your underlying problem. If you really want to change, look at yourself until you see the reason that caused you to fail in previous attempts.

The next exercise is to confess that your weakness will no longer control you. Say, "Laziness will not control me," or "unawareness will not control me," or "the desire to give up and die will not control me," or "avoidance of the issue will no longer control me," or "anger will no longer control me."

There are two areas of physical fitness to deal with: eating nutritious food, and choosing the right exercise program. There are so many books, tapes, and information available on these subjects that I am not going to try to give you a complete food or exercise plan. I will, however, give you some thoughts to help in the renewing of the spirit of your mind in these areas.

As you *apply* yourself to the diet or exercise programs you choose, you will begin to see results. You must have the right thoughts, the right attitude, before any program will work for you.

You can make your own program by writing down one thing you could do to improve your diet instead of revising everything you eat. Maybe cutting out coffee, sugar, or salt would make a big difference in your life. Determine to deal with that one thing first. Go through the process of change that you learned in the first part of this book. The heartfelt desire to change will give you the strength to overcome the habit or the addiction.

Write down one thing you can do every day to improve your physical condition. Perhaps it will be to go for a walk, to do a few simple exercises in your bedroom, or ride an exercise bike for five minutes. Find one simple thing you can do to start becoming physically fit.

Get your calendar and write down those plans for each day for the next thirty days. Then make yourself follow that plan. Do not think about whether you want to do it. Do not ask yourself if there have been any changes or results — just follow your plan! You will begin to see positive results after thirty days. You will find yourself feeling better, even looking better. This is the beginning of a physical fitness program that can make a tremendous difference in your life.

Make this your confession:

1. My priorities are in order — faith, fitness, family, fellowship, finances, and fun.

2. My mind is free from worry and is growing in knowledge.

3. My body is getting more healthy, stronger, and active every day.

As you apply yourself to these principles, the spirit of your mind in this area will begin to be renewed. By taking time to examine your life and plan changes, you will enter into a new realm of mental and physical fitness. You will begin to enjoy life in a much greater way.

7

Finances: Your Golden Opportunity

I wrote earlier about putting too much time, energy, and focus on finances; however, finances obviously are important. In this chapter, I want to give you some practical steps that will help you reach financial goals without overemphasizing the desire or search for money.

If you were granted three wishes, more than likely, one of them would be for money. Hoping for "wishes to come true," however, is not reality. Your financial stability cannot be based on wishful thinking. What brings financial stability is exchanging poverty thinking for prosperity thinking.

The first thing to realize is that *financial prosperity starts in the mind.* This is the hardest step for anyone to understand, and it is the most important point. If you do not understand this, the rest of this chapter is going to be of little benefit to you.

The reason it is so hard for most of us to understand that financial prosperity is a way of thinking is because we are convinced that more money would bring happiness. Yet that is a lie which has so many people caught in a trap. More money is not the answer to our problems, no matter how strongly we are convinced that it is. That is a fallacy.

Many of us have increased greatly in our incomes over the years, yet we are in the same condition we were when our incomes were considerably smaller. Having more money will not change your circumstances or solve your problems. The way you think about money is controlling the way you handle and experience the money you have.

Here are four stories of people I know that prove this point.

Ray, Jim, Frank, and Bill

Ray was raised in a nice home, went to college, and got a degree in history which he never used. He began working in a drugstore as a teenager making $1.50 an hour. After twelve years, he had grown to the salary of about $6 an hour. With two children and a wife, to put it simply, Ray was poor. He had scraped enough money together to buy a small house in a poor section of town. Every month, he spent every dime making his house payment, keeping an old truck running, buying food for his family, and just barely getting by. *He was poor.*

He tried doing different things. In fact, he eventually went to work for one of the drug companies that supplied products to the store where he had first worked. Yet, he was still just barely making ends meet. His salary had gotten up to about $1,500 a month. "Barely getting by" was his testimony.

He came to our church in Seattle and began listening to the teaching about renewing the spirit of our minds. He began to change the way he thought. That, of course, caused him to change on the job. He became a different kind of employee, a better worker, and his company offered him a better position — a higher paying job in another city. But he had become a part of the church. He was enjoying the teaching and changes he was experiencing and didn't want to move. So, he turned down the job and was without work for two months.

Now you might think, "Boy, Ray has gone from bad to worse. Here is a fellow that was poor. Now he has no job at all."

In reality, what was happening was that he was getting ready to make some great strides forward because he was changing his thinking. Remember, when you begin to change, there may be some things from which you will have to dissociate yourself.

Ray dissociated from his past and the people with whom he had been involved. Soon he was part of a new staff, a new company, involved with a new position, and making more money than he ever had before. Today, he owns a brand new home, drives beautiful cars, and his income is in the top ten percent of the whole nation. His children and wife are blessed. They are very prosperous people.

How did that all happen? Was it because he got a better education? A lucky break? An inheritance? No, what happened is that Ray changed his thinking.

Jim came to me several years ago, more than $30,000 in debt. I am not talking about debt from a house mortgage. I am talking about "consumer debt" — credit cards, and so forth. He did not know where his money had gone. He had taken out loans and obtained credit cards from just about every credit union and store in town, and yet had nothing to show for it.

He had hocked everything he could to pay off the bills. He even sold his house to try to catch up, but that did not help much. He was in a very bad financial spot.

Soon the government took over his finances, garnished his wages, told him what he could spend his money on, and every month, his paycheck went to a federal court that distributed the money he made.

However, Jim began to change his thinking and renew his mind. Within a short period of time, less than half the time the government had said it would take, he was completely out of debt and making more money than he ever had before. Things seemed to be going great.

But one thing had not happened. Jim had not completely renewed his mind. He had only changed a few ideas. Although he was making twice as much as before, soon the debt began to come back, just like some people lose a few pounds and then gain the weight back. As soon as he realized what was happening, he began to renew his mind even more. He made a complete change, and although his income did not again increase, his financial condition stabilized. He no longer had to struggle with the pressure of always being in debt.

I am going to call the third man **Frank**. He is one of those people who always seems to have a good job with enough money. Yet at the end of every month, he has spent all he had. He is not behind, but he has nothing left. He did not plan properly. He spent some money on fixing up his house, then he borrowed even more. So his family, for several years, has barely made ends meet each month. They have to pay off the excess construction bills on the house. He has developed a lifestyle of "barely getting by." It does not matter if his income increases $500 or $2,000 a month. At the end of the month, he is at zero again.

There is one more person I want to tell you about. I am going to call him **Bill**. Bill had inherited a business and a large amount of money from his father. And he spent all his time trying to hang onto it.

When I got to know Bill, he had more than enough money, three cars in the garage, a beautiful waterfront home. Yet, to hear him talk, he was about to "go under" at any time. He was constantly saving, guarding, and protecting his money. He was making sure he did not lose the money that had been left to him. He spent his days worrying that his friends might be trying to get his money. He has gone through two bad marriages and is working right now on the third. Things are tough, although he has more than enough money. His greed and his fear of losing his inheritance was destroying his life.

I am sure that you have seen similarities between these stories and your own financial situation. It is not the *money* that has to change; it is not the economic system that has to change; it is not your boss, company, or job that has to change. What needs to change is your thinking about money. Then your finances will stabilize.

Seven Attitudes of a Prosperity Mentality

Get your pencil and paper again. Write down what you think about finances. Do you think:

- "I never have enough"?

- "I'm always trying to get more"?

- "I have to save every dime I get"?

- "Easy come, easy go"?

- "If I could just get another loan, everything would be all right"?

Briefly, in two or three sentences, write down how you think about money.

If you have written down all sorts of positive thoughts about money, but you have had financial difficulties in the past, you have just lied to yourself! It is impossible to have positive thinking about money and be going through negative experiences. All of us may face tough times, but if your finances have been in bad shape for a long time, it is because you have some bad thinking. You must be honest with yourself and face the negative thinking you have about money and finances. Being honest with the way you think is the first step to making some changes.

God wants all of us to prosper financially. He wants us to enjoy the good of the land (Is. 1:19), to leave an inheritance to our children (Prov. 13:22), to give to the poor (Deut. 15:7), and he wants us to give to the work of the ministry (Gal. 6:6). To do God's will on the earth, we need to begin to prosper financially. He will help us reprogram our minds in this area so we can do His work on this earth.

Here are seven concepts that, if you will speak them out loud until you believe them, will turn your thinking around.

1. I can manage money. I can control it, and use it properly. I am not foolish with money. I do not waste it.

2. There is more than enough money available to me. I am not limited or held back by "the system." I am not stopped by the past, by my education, or by anything else.

3. I use money wisely, invest it wisely, manage it wisely, earn it wisely and save it wisely.

4. I can save money. It does not slip through my fingers. It is not gone at the end of the week or the month. I save money. I pay myself before I pay the rest of the world. I can save money.

5. I am growing in financial prosperity. I am increasing monthly. I am not struggling; I am not barely making it; I am not getting farther and farther behind. *Every month, I increase.*

6. The economy of this world does not control me. My job does not control my finances. My boss does not control my finances. The government does not control my finances. The IRS does not control my finances.

7. I am a liberal giver. I enjoy giving. I enjoy giving to my friends. I enjoy giving to the poor. I love to give to ministries. I am not selfish. I am not greedy. I am a liberal giver.

As you think and say these things and make them a part of your normal thinking, God will help you change your life. You will begin to find the opportunities necessary to turn around your present financial condition.

Six Ways to a Healthy Cash Flow

These six steps will help you manage your money and will bring you into a pattern of growth:

1. You must know what your current financial condition is.

2. You must know where your money is going.

3. You must decrease your expenses to 80 percent of your income.

4. You must establish a monthly budget and follow it.

5. You must begin to save 10 percent.

6. You must begin giving 10 percent, if you do not already do this.

To do the first two steps, you may have to write down everything you spend for thirty days. We have found in our financial counseling that many people do not know how up to half their money is spent. They go through the convenience stores, out to fast-food restaurants, down to the mall, and it is as if money just sort of disappears. So, you may have to write down every penny for thirty days to see what your situation is and where your money is going.

In order to get your expenses down to 80 percent of your take-home pay, you may have to cut back on grocery spending, recreation, clothes, or other areas. But decrease that monthly expense however you can, if you want to get your finances in shape.

Next, make a plan. People who live "by the seat of their pants," who live by whatever happens to come along, usually do not know where they are going. They do not know where they are or even how they got there. So, work out a plan for your finances. A budget is simply a money plan.

Begin to save 10 percent. Pay yourself before you pay the landlord, the utility bills, and everyone else. Save that money and only use it for very special asset-increasing investments — for a new home, a car, or special things.

Then start giving 10 percent. Give to your church and other ministries. Money given is like seed sown in a field — the farmer knows he is not going to reap a harvest until he plants some seed. Start planting *your* financial seed.

My wife and I have been able to increase what we give to more than 30 percent. Our goal is to continue to give up to 90 percent, so that we can live on 10 percent of our income. Think of the freedom, peace of mind, and happiness in knowing you are giving most of your income to help others and still living a comfortable, prosperous life. Be a liberal giver, and you will find great freedom in your finances.

As your personal worth increases, your finances will increase. When you do more than you are paid for, you will start getting paid more. When you are worth more than you are paid, you will start getting paid more. You need to increase your personal value. Increase what you are worth to your company and to society around you.

Take some time to exercise the imagination we talked about earlier and write down what you *could be worth*. Write down ten ways in which you could be worth more on your job or in your community. This might be to improve your self-discipline, to improve your efficiency, to improve yourself through education. As you increase your personal worth, be looking for new opportunities. Do not get stuck in a rut. Do not get stuck in a maintenance position. As you increase in value, keep your eyes open for better jobs with better incomes.

At the same time, remember to keep your priorities in proper order. If your priorities get out of balance, then all these other things will not work. Your life will get out of balance again, and you will begin to struggle. Remember your priorities.

As you change what you think and what you say, your financial situation will begin to change in your life. Don't spend half your life hoping for "a break," for some "lucky" event that will change your fortune. Your thinking has a lot more to do with your life than luck.

8

Relationships: A Change of Heart

Your relationships with others determine the activities of your life, the success and harmony of your marriage, and the security or the promotion you experience in your job. I would like to begin by giving a couple of examples of men I have worked with in the past.

The first man is Don. He was a good worker and very well-qualified. He was very efficient and knew how to do the job right. Yet his attitude was so bad he never got along with others in the company, and he never got along with management. He figured they were stupid and did not know how to do things right. If they would just leave him alone, he would get it done better than they could. He did not get along too well with his fellow workers, because most of them were not as efficient as he, and he made sure they knew that!

He was constantly out of a job and looking for work, although he was one of the best in the field. Because of his poor relationships, he did not have job security. He never moved up the ladder in the companies with which he worked. His relationships kept him from being promoted and many times cost him his job.

Another person I spent some time with years ago, I will call "Dick." Dick was a very good student. He took extra classes and really studied for the job he was assigned to do. He worked well and never bothered anyone. In fact, he was happiest if you never talked to him, and he never talked to you. He would just put his entire focus on his work while shutting out the rest of the world. He worked like that all day, every day.

He did a very good job, but he had little or no contact with those around him. He had some of the same problems as Don! If there was a cutback, or a change in responsibilities, he was first to go, or the last to be promoted. Because he was not involved with the people around him, fellow workers and management did not know him. And when people do not know you, they do not trust you. Because of a lack of relationships, he was hindered in his progress through life.

One of these men was hindered by developing bad relationships through bad attitudes; the other was hindered by developing no relationships at all.

In my own life, I can look back and see that in different jobs and positions, I overcame a lack of training and ability by having good relationships with the people around me. Fellow workers with whom I had built relationships would help me in those areas in which I lacked experience or training. At the same time, management was able to believe that I had potential and would promote me because of good relationships. They felt they knew me and knew what I would and would not do.

What is the condition of your relationships with those around you? Think about the people you work with, live with, and with whom you associate most often.

- Are your relationships rewarding and fulfilling?

- Are they weak, stagnant and boring?

- Are you excited to be around the people that you know? Or do you just put up with them?

Let's take a look at some steps you can take to build exciting, fulfilling and rewarding relationships with others.

Do Not Try To Change Others — Change Yourself!

I am sure that you cannot change other people — but you *can* change yourself. The beginning of a good relationship is not to worry about what others are doing. You can make yourself a better friend, a better business associate or a better church member by building the qualities and characteristics for positive relationships into your own life.

Here are six qualities to consider in order to have strong relationships:

1. Be encouraging to others.

2. Be interesting.

3. Be exciting.

4. Be giving and generous.

5. Be honest.

6. Be there when they need you.

These characteristics will begin to make you the kind of person others want to be around. When you are that kind of person, you are on your way to experiencing exciting, fun-filled relationships.

Five Levels of Relationships

There are five levels of relationship, and few people go beyond the second level.

The first level is *acquaintance*. We bump into some people now and then. We know their names and a little bit about them. When we see them, we make small talk. We "shoot the breeze," talk about the weather, the job, the stock market, the latest television show, how our families are doing. We are acquainted with them.

The second level is a *working relationship*. We get along well in the workplace. We are with each other daily. We ask about the family and things to do with work.

The third level is *friendship*. Friends are ones you will give to. If they need $500, and you have it, you would give it to them without thinking twice about it, because you are good friends. Perhaps you travel together, sit and fellowship together, talk about some things you keep private from acquaintances.

The fourth level is *intimacy*. This is a *close* friend. On this level, you are willing to share any part of your life. You talk about problems you may be having with a spouse or a teenage son. You are willing to let them know your fears, hopes, or dreams. There is nothing you would hide from someone with whom you have this kind of relationship.

The fifth level is *marriage*, or total union the way God intended it to be. The marriage relationship is "oneness." Your spouse knows everything about you, and you know everything about your spouse. There is no lie, nothing hidden, nothing covered up. You are able to discuss anything and everything. Your life is one with theirs.

Now you can understand why I said most people never go beyond level two, even in their marriages. Many people do not even have friendships with their spouses.

Hindrances to Intimacy

Think about each of the following five reasons and be honest with yourself as to whether any of them are keeping you from having good, satisfying relationships.

1. The feeling that you do not need intimate friends. You really do not want to share your life and be intimate with others. This is a great hindrance to relationships in our society.

2. You have a fear of others knowing the real you. You have the thought that if they really knew you, they would not like you. So you pretend to be the kind of person you think they would like, and you end up being artificial and shallow.

3. Things in your past that you do not want others to know — perhaps an abortion, a bankruptcy, a past divorce, a business problem.

4. You think you do not have time for friends. You do not have time to talk, to get together with others. You are too busy. Other things are more important.

5. You wait for other people to reach out and be your friend. You wait for them to call, to set up the engagement, to reach out. Waiting for others to take the first step is a great hindrance to intimacy in our relationships.

Your next step is to look at yourself honestly and write down the things that hinder you in this area.

- Is it the feeling that you do not need them?

- Is it a fear of others knowing you?

- Is it past things you feel you must cover up?

- Is it not taking time to get to know people?

- Is it waiting for others to make the relationship work?

The next thing you must do is decide how you are going to overcome these hindrances. Decide that you are going to take the first step and begin to build positive relationships. Decide you are not going to let your job and other activities steal from your relationships. Decide that you are going to be bold and no longer be afraid of people getting to know who you are. Taking the risk of being rejected is part of life. If one person rejects you; the next one may not. If other people reject you, that is *their* problem, not yours.

By admitting your hindrances, and by taking steps of action, you are on your way to building exciting, fulfilling, and rewarding relationships with others.

Say these things out loud right now:

"I admit to the hindrances in my relationships."

"I have decided to overcome them."

"I am taking positive action to build positive relationships."

Five Keys for Strong Relationships

First of all, there is *communication*. Do you share yourself openly and freely? Do you share your thoughts and feelings; what excites you and what brings you down? Do you share your good days and bad days? When people challenge or confront you, do you just become quiet? Are you an open, free, expressive, outgoing person? Are you quiet, withdrawn, and do not say much, even when people ask? What is the condition of your ability to communicate? On a scale of one to ten, rate yourself with one being weak and ten being strong.

Number two is *honesty.* Are you an honest person? Do you tell people when you are having a bad day? Do you share when you are feeling down? Do you let them know when you have failed? Are you honest with the negative things of your life, as well as the positive? Do you hide, cover, excuse, and rationalize your actions? Do you tell the truth? Remember that to lie by omission is also a sin. Give yourself a rating in the area of honesty in relationships.

Number three is *encouragement*. This is so important in relationships. People want and need to be encouraged. Do you try to lift others? Do you try to make people feel good and be happy when they are around you? Are you a "lift" in the office or a "wet blanket"? Are you spreading joy and happiness, or doom and gloom? Give yourself a rating in this area.

Number four is *giving*. Giving is a big part in building strong relationships. Do you always want things your way? Or are you willing to give? In simple things like going to a restaurant for lunch, is it always your choice, or do you let others choose as well? At dinner with friends, do you get out your calculator and figure out how much each owes? Or do you just give what you can and maybe cover someone else's meal? Are you a giving, generous person? Do you worry about other people taking advantage of you, or are you willing to give? Rate yourself in this area.

Number five is *listening*. Do you really know those around you? Do you ask questions about their lives, their feelings, their thoughts, their ideas? Do you listen? If we could compare your jaw muscles to your ear muscles, are you working your jaws and exercising your mouth more than your ears? There is a saying, "I have one mouth and two ears, so I'll listen twice as much as I talk." How would you rate yourself in *really listening* and caring about the people around you? Give yourself a "ten" if you are interested in others and are careful to listen. Give yourself a "one" if you talk all the time and do not care about what they have to say.

Take these five keys and examine the areas where your rating was low. All of us can improve in each area. In the areas where you were weak, begin working to bring that rating up. For example, if you gave yourself a low rating in giving, begin to give without worrying about being paid back. If your record at encouraging was not very strong, write down some things you can say to uplift and encourage others. As you follow through on some of these things, you will begin to see a change in your relationships.

Finally, let's see how building relationships is really a process of sowing and reaping. Every word you say is a seed; every gesture of kindness is a seed; and everything you do with and for the people around you is a seed. And that seed is going to grow up and produce fruit. It will either produce good fruit or bad fruit. If you will begin to regularly sow good seed in others, you will start to control the quality of your relationships.

Say these things out loud, over and over, until you believe them:

"I care about the people around me."

"I am willing to share myself intimately."

"I love others, as I love myself."

The way you treat others determines whether they will work with you or against you. Good relationships do not "just happen." You must apply yourself to developing them. Imagine the joy you will feel when you experience the true friendship of other people in your life.

Casey Treat is an outstanding minister, author and motivational speaker. He pastors one of the largest churches in the Pacific Northwest, Christian Faith Center, in Seattle, Washington. He also hosts his own daily television program as well as weekly programs which are broadcast in several cities in the United States.

Casey Treat is the founder of Dominion University in Seattle and an adjunct professor at Oral Roberts University in Tulsa. He serves on the board of directors of Church Growth International founded by Dr. Paul Yonggi Cho in Seoul, Korea, and is a co-founding trustee of Charismatic Bible Ministries. He holds Success Through Excellence seminars for business people.

Traveling extensively each year, Casey Treat speaks at large conventions and churches, and there is a worldwide distribution of his books and taped teaching series.

Casey Treat resides in the Seattle area with his wife, Wendy, and their children.

For a complete catalog of books and tape series
by Casey Treat, write to:

Casey Treat
P. O. Box 98800
Seattle, WA 98198

Please include your prayer requests
and comments when you write.